JAMES DEAN

THE QUEST
FOR AN OSCAR

JAMES TURIELLO

published by

a sandy beach

LAS VEGAS, NEVADA

Published in the USA by
A Sandy Beach
Las Vegas, Nevada 89120

ISBN-10: 0692081828
ISBN-13: 978-0692081822

Designed by duffincreative.com

Printed in the United States of America

Table of Contents

Pirates, Buccaneers, men of the sea....Captain Kidd, Henry Morgan, Blackbeard, Calico Jack, Francois L'Olonnais, Sir Francis Drake....the rougher the seas, the smoother we sail....an ode....

To Errol Flynn and James Dean....

Foreword

"Dream as if you'll live forever. Live as if you'll die today."

WHERE DOES ONE BEGIN to describe the unique and memorable performances that the one and only James Dean created on the big screen. The word created has to be used because Jimmy in his own style actually managed to do what each and every actor before or after him strived for. As you know Jimmy only made three motion pictures and then he was gone. The three characters that he brought to life were all by his design and craftsmanship distinctive and memorable. It would be difficult to select one to evaluate and submit that character, that role, that performance for Oscar consideration. This book is also unique and special because it will evaluate the three performances by looking at the most finite details that went into the character development. The book is not a biography but it will contain photos relative to the roles described in order to visualize the argument and provide justification of recognition. There will be absolutely no doubt that after the reader completes the book the reader will agree that still one more great actor was overlooked and should now be recognized with an Oscar. Jimmy is ever present and the legacy he left behind is timeless. So let's get started we have some very cool places to visit, Salinas Valley in California, where we catch a glimpse of Cal Trask. Then we race to suburban Los Angeles and are shocked by the rebel Jim Stark. Finally our journey places us in a desert somewhere in the biggest state, Texas and are confronted by not one but two Jett Rink's. One is young and rebellious and the other is old and without reservation.

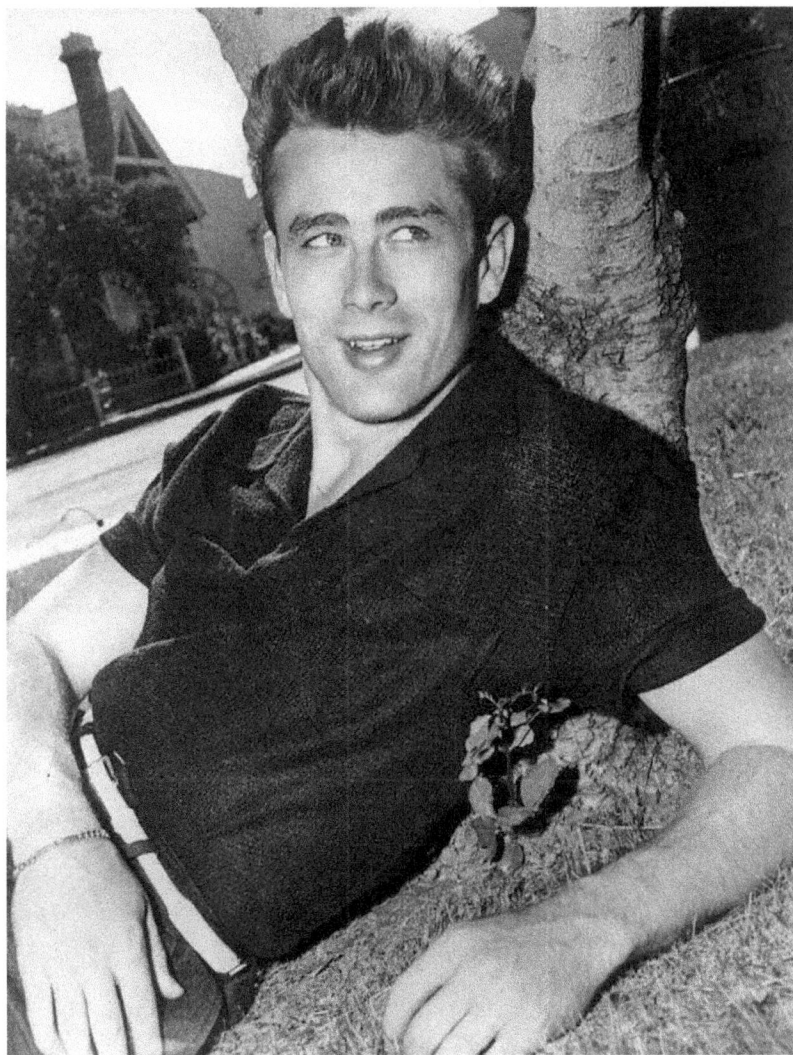

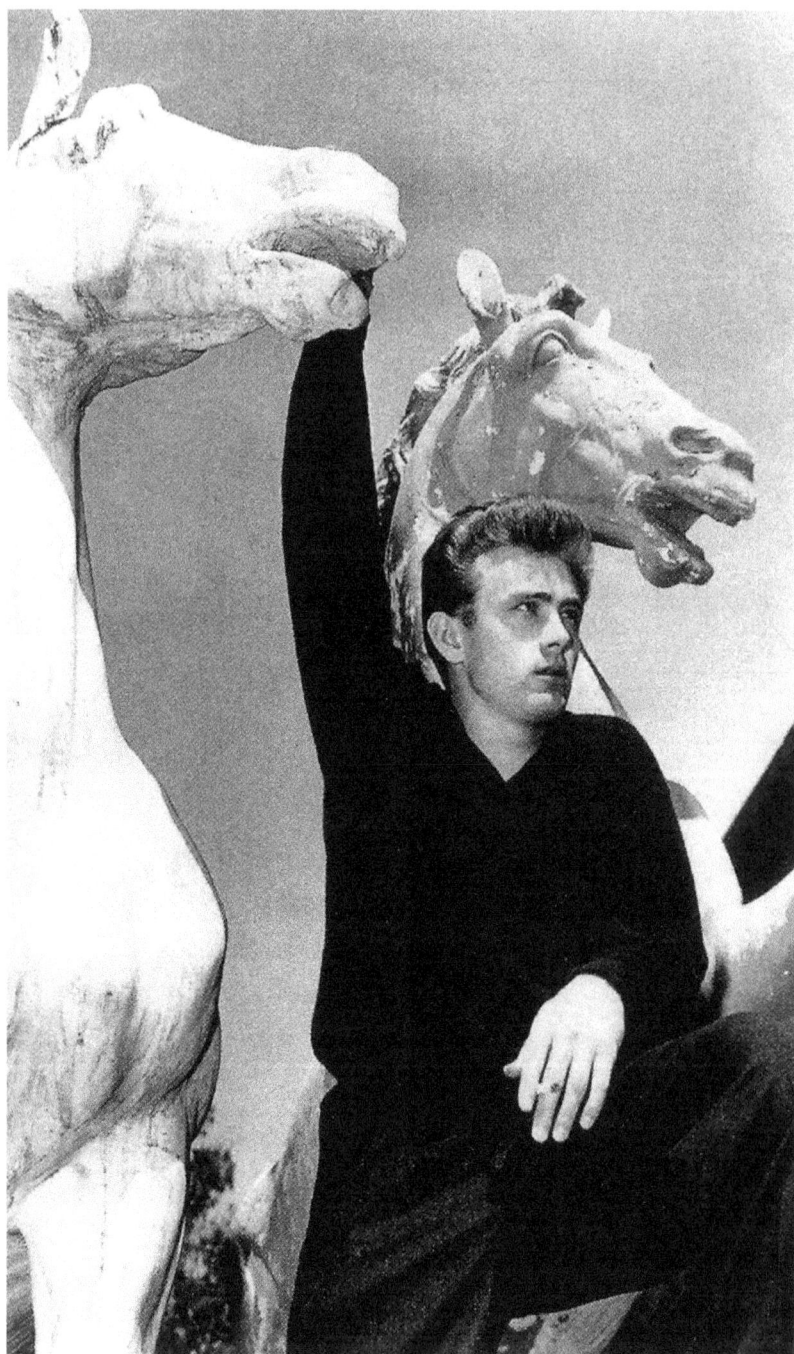

CHAPTER 1

In the Beginning

Jimmy jumps from a tiny screen to a gigantic one

"I don't know how good a lawyer I might have become, but I'm still young and if I flop as an actor, I'll certainly return to law study."

THE QUEST FOR JIMMY'S OSCAR began at UCLA when a very determined James Dean took part in what can only be described as a gigantic casting lottery which had over three hundred and fifty applicants. He was thrilled and delighted when he landed the role of Malcolm in "Macbeth". It was evident from all of the recollections of this very early acting endeavor that Jimmy was going to be unique if not special. The other actors in the production really didn't get along with him and most if not all recalled his strange habit of 'doing his own thing'. For example, Jimmy read his lines and acted out his part as if he was completely alone on the stage. That trait carried off the stage as well because in the dorm he usually spent all his free time alone drawing sketches.

1

Here we have a very strong indication of the greatness that was to follow in each and every role regardless of the size of the role that he undertook. Acting was the most important thing in his life even though he was still in college where most individuals were learning a profession. Jimmy wasn't one for the books and he was failing all of his courses. If he wasn't drawing sketches or trying out for roles in college productions he was in Hollywood looking for television or even movie work. It most likely was his indifference that led to Jimmy failing to get a role in a forthcoming UCLA production of "Dark of the Moon " as Witch Boy. He desperately wanted that role and when he was looked over Jimmy left college and made his way to of all places New York. It should be noted that exactly as Errol Flynn did early in his career Jimmy joined an informal workshop in acting coached by James Whitmore a very successful stage and Hollywood actor. Whitmore encouraged his students to use their imagination and for Jimmy that was virtually tailor made, he was a total non-conformist. The approach was to find out what you wanted as an artist something that was a lasting influence on Jimmy's career. It was James Whitmore who saw greatness in Jimmy and convinced him to leave Hollywood and go to New York. It was a gamble on his part but Jimmy took the advice and several years later he stated that it was James Whitmore who was the most influential person in his life. New York was very different than Hollywood for young actors because of all the Television productions being produced. Remember this is the 1950's and television was taking off like a comet and for every casting role you had in Hollywood, in New York there were fifty. Those were great odds and when you had a mentor like Whitmore coupled with your relentless drive, roles would come easy. It was during the years 1951 to 1955 that James Dean acted in a total of thirty-four television shows. When you re-visit these productions as raw as they were Jimmy stands out in each and every one. Keep in mind that most of these productions were live TV and once you went before the cameras you only had one shot to get it right. Jimmy thrived on that spontaneity, and it most certainly got him noticed in a big way. It is important to take a closer look at most of these half hour or hourly shows and get a true feel of the way Jimmy attacks the role completely different than all of the other cast members. It was a time when if you wanted to be noticed by Hollywood the new media of television was where almost all of the motion picture stars got their breaks. When you examine these productions that James Dean acted in there will be several other big name stars who like Jimmy were virtual unknowns at the time.

When James Dean took on the role of Cal Trask in *East of Eden* the only work he had on his resume before the camera was the television dramas. There are only a handful of actors who get nominated for an Oscar with their very first performance. Jimmy was so good that most critics were already comparing him to Marlon Brando. That comparison would stay with Jimmy for the rest of his short career. His performance was one that introduced Jimmy to the motion picture audience. He was embraced by them and he was nominated for an Oscar in Best Actor in a Leading Role category. The winner was Ernest Borgnine for his role in *Marty*. Jimmy was up against some of Hollywood's greatest actors as well as some of those actors greatest roles. The actors and the movies they starred in were; James Cagney for *Love Me or Leave Me*. Then a most outstanding and true to life performance by Frank Sinatra in *The Man with the Golden Arm*. Finally Spencer Tracy in *Bad Day at Black Rock*. As you can see the competition and the roles were all not only great but some of the most memorable of all time. The Cal Trask character was unique and not an easy one to master by any means. The entire movie was shot in a short ten weeks. The producer and director was the iconic Elia Kazan. He was extremely focused on realism and the smallest of details. He even sent Jimmy off to Palm Springs to gain some weight and get a deep tan so that he looked like a "real" farm boy. Dean hated getting a tan, having his hair cut, and drinking a pint of cream a day to put on pounds. In still another effort to insure that Jimmy's interpretation of the Cal Trask character was almost perfect Elia Kazan did the unthinkable. He was well aware that James Deans relationship with his real life father was tempestuous. Kazan decided to arrange a meeting between the two Deans and it turned out to be rewarding on his part. He made Dean visit his father in Los Angeles where he was living at the time. What he witnessed shocked him at first. The elder

Dean treated Jimmy very badly even though Jimmy only wanted to please him. As time went by and Kazan got to know Jimmy better, Elia Kazan saw how the broken relationship between the father and the son had instilled in him a great deal of anger. He realized it was because of frustrated love, the key element to the character of Cal Trask. Mr. Kazan later stated, "It was the most unique and interesting piece of casting I've ever done in my life." *East of Eden* the movie was based on the John Steinbeck novel of the same name. The novel was well received and soon after it was released made it to the number one on the best seller list. An interesting side note to the novel is that today it still sells over 50,000 copies a year.

CHAPTER 2

Broadway, Times Square and Washington Heights

IF YOU DIDN'T HAVE THE GOOD FORTUNE to live in a big city like New York then most likely going to the movies each and every Saturday morning was a unique treasure you missed. There are several reasons why this is true and to illustrate why here is the scenario. I lived in the uptown section of Manhattan called Washington Heights. It has a very special history and is the neighborhood in the northern portion of New York City borough of Manhattan. This area is named for Fort Washington, a fortification constructed at the highest point on Manhattan Island by Continental Army troops during the American Revolutionary War, to defend the area from the British forces. Washington Heights is bordered by Harlem to the south, along 155 Street, Inwood to the north along Hillside Avenue, the Hudson River to the west, and the Harlem

River and Coogan's Bluff to the east. Movies and movie making have always been a major part of the history of Washington Heights.

- In the film *Citizen Kane*, Jedidiah Leland is spending the remainder of his life in the fictitious "Huntington Memorial Hospital" on 180th Street.
- The film *Coogan's Bluff* features a scene where Clint Eastwood chases the criminal he is to bring back to Arizona through the Cloisters in upper Manhattan, Washington Heights.
- The film *How to Marry a Millionaire* features the George Washington Bridge entering into Washington Heights when Waldo Brewster, a grumpy businessman (Fred Clark), and Loco Dempsey (Betty Grable), driving back into Manhattan from the "Elks Lodge", are pulled over by motorcycle cops so the bridge commission can recognize "the lucky couple" as the occupants of the bridge's 50th millionth vehicle.
- The Showtime series *Weeds* features Washington Heights as the location of Nancy Botwin's halfway house in Season 7.
- The film *American Gangster*, was filmed in some sections of Washington Heights.

These are just a few of the ties the area called Washington Heights has to the media of visual arts, namely motion pictures. The most unique part and connection to movies in general was the great amount of movie theaters situated on almost every corner. Most people outside of New York are familiar with Broadway and Times Square and consider that section as the hub of movie and entertainment venues. However, Washington Heights had numerous movie theaters and a few are considered as true movie palaces. It was at one of the many majestic movie theaters that I saw James Dean second movie, *Rebel Without a Cause*. Each and every Saturday morning me and a group of my friends would meet and go to one of these movie theaters. The day began quite early, because the first movie began at approximately 9:00AM and the entire experience sometimes lasted until five or even six o'clock in the evening. How about watching not one but two first length movies,

GEORGE STEVENS
Giganten
EDNA FERBER
ELIZABETH TAYLOR · ROCK HUDSON
JAMES DEAN
CARROL BAKER

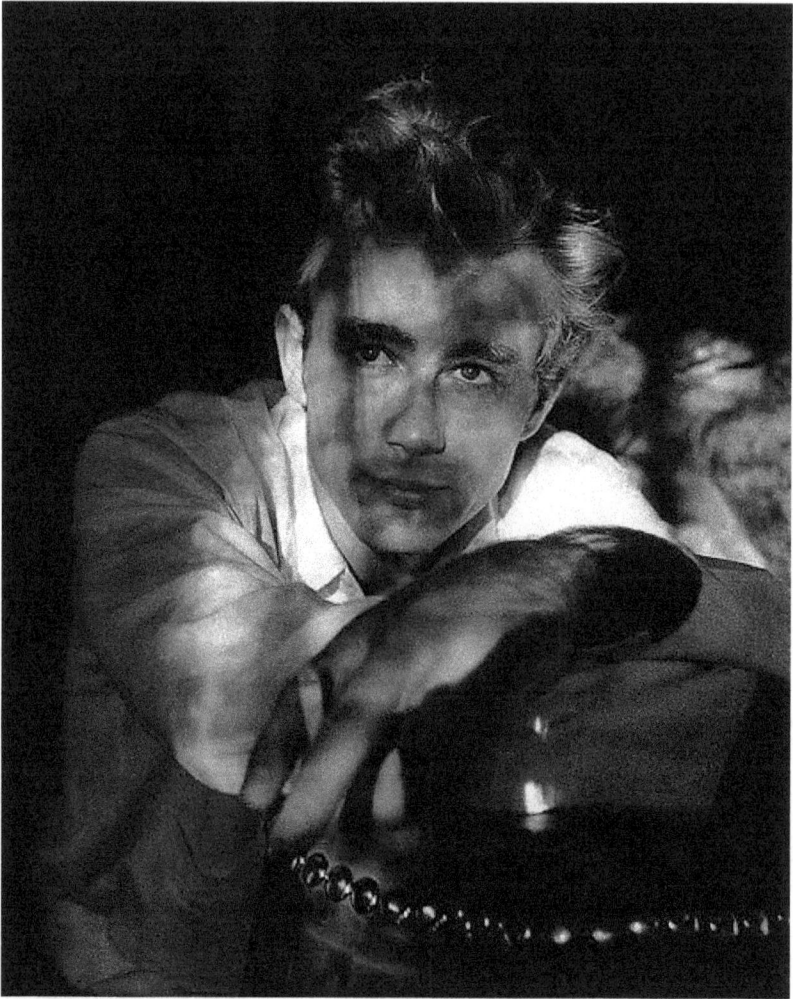

five cartoons and an episode of some serial. The serial was always extremely entertaining and had a cliffhanger ending. Some of the best Saturday morning serials were *Tim Tyler's Luck*, *Flash Gordon's Trip to Mars* and *Don Winslow of the Coast Guard*. All of the movie theaters in my neighborhood except one ran the aforementioned program. On special occasions these theaters even ran a triple feature Saturday extravaganza. There was the Lane Theater, the Gem Theater and the Empress Theater all on the same block. The Empress Theater even had a pipe organ even though it was the smallest theater of these three. Only one block from these three theaters was The Heights Theater which specialized in showing first run foreign movies. A half block from The Heights Theater was my closest move house, only one short block from where I lived. This theater was one of my favorites, The RKO Coliseum. It was the second biggest movie theater that I went to and was bordered by two other great landmarks. Across the street on opposite corners was Nedicks, a fast food franchise that was famous for its hot dogs and the best orange drink. The other was Bickfords cafeteria, a place where the food was in little glass windows and you inserted the proper amount of money and the door would open to allow you to get your meal. It was a very unique time to live in a special area of the city. However, within walking distance about five city blocks was the pinnacle of movie theaters not only in Washington Heights but in the entire United States. The movie theater was the Loew's 175th Street and it was the last of the "Wonder Theatres" erected between 1925 and 1930. These Wonder Theatres were so named because of their extravagant design and because they housed the twin chamber, seven-story high Robert Morton Wonder organ. The theaters were originally placed in strategic areas in the metropolitan area to provide Vaudeville shows. After the complete decline of Vaudeville and the growing popularity of moving pictures the theaters were quickly converted to a deluxe movie house. Almost every Saturday morning it was customary for me and a couple of close friends to take in a double feature. The movies were each preceded by the aforementioned cartoons and a chapter of a cliffhanger serial. On one of these adventures as I like to remember them as, I had my very first encounter of a James Dean movie. The mood I was in that day as well as the weather was just perfect for going to my favorite movie house, the great Loew's 175th Street. The sky was overcast and it was not raining hard, just a very misty drizzle. As I passed the familiar stores on more than one occasion I was greeted by several store owners who customarily stood outside when they had no customers. The first one I walked by was Mr. Switzman's candy store. It was quite small but had a soda fountain that had 6 seats and he made the best chocolate egg cream in all of Manhattan. A few blocks from Mr. Switzman's was Milties Clothing

JAMES DEAN
LA FUREUR DE VIVRE
un film de
NICHOLAS RAY
JAMES DEAN
"LA FUREUR DE VIVRE"
NATALIE WOOD

store, old man Milty had the coolest up to date styles and I was the only teenager who got his clothes there, it was too loud and garish for the rest of my friends. Then there was Hobbyland, another place that I was the only one of my clique that bought there. Almost every week I bought a plastic model car or plane kit. Then just before the movie house was Goldberg's Stamp Shop, it also was a place I spent my money in on a weekly basis. Finally adjacent to the movie house was Heights Records, a great place to buy all the latest 45's, which cost about 39 cents a real bargain even for those days. I was going by myself because it was the Jewish holiday of Yom Kippur, a very high holy day, most if not all of the guys and girls in my neighborhood were Jewish. The movies on the marquee were *Tarzan's Hidden Jungle and Rebel Without a Cause.* Both of the stars names were also on the marquee and to be honest it was Gordon Scott, Tarzan, and not James Dean who I was looking forward to seeing on this particular Saturday. The ticket booth had absolutely no line and I guessed the Jewish holiday was responsible. Upon entering the lobby and making my way to the concession stand it was obvious that today would be a quiet one. Usually on Saturday matinee days the entire theater is packed and at times the noise does become a factor. The seats were oversized and sported red velvet cushions. Before the first movie started it was cartoon time. In the 1950's the big cartoon titles were Popeye, Casper The Friendly Ghost and all the Loony Tunes. That Saturday there were six cartoons and of course a chapter of one of my favorite cliffhangers, *Tim Tyler's Luck.* Then after some great trailers and a reminder to visit the snack bar, it was time for the main attraction, *Tarzan's Hidden Jungle.* There have been several actors that have played Tarzan but Gordon Scott was the closest to the Edgar Rice Burroughs character. Gordon had a great upper body but the rest of his physique was indicative of what you might envision Tarzan looked like. There is a very interesting side note regarding Gordon Scott. He was discovered at a swimming pool and at the time was a professional body builder with no formal acting training. This version of Tarzan was Gordon's film debut. It was one of the best Tarzan movies that I ever viewed and when the movie ended I felt it should have been the second feature because how could the James Dean

movie come close. As was my custom I went to the snack bar and purchased two boxes of Bon-Bons. These were very special small chocolate covered ice cream treats. It was evident right after the first scene with Jimmy in the police station that I was watching greatness and as the movie progressed so did the entire audience. In reality everyone in the theater was completely engulfed in the special drama right up on the big screen. Jimmy had captured the audience like no other actor before or since and this movie was only the second he starred in so far. Jimmy proved to me that day that only great performances would follow and I looked forward to what I knew he was more than capable of delivering, he was truly one of a kind. How ironic that my enthusiasm regarding the prospect of seeing a Tarzan movie with a virtual unknown cast in the role of Tarzan, was completely overshadowed by James Dean. As I left the theater, and walked down the extremely long lobby corridor, I stopped briefly to look at the many 8x10 photos that were located on both walls. In the early days of movies, it was commonplace to display these very special photos as you entered the movie house. Today it is a long forgotten tradition that made going to the movies extra special. I gazed back at the giant poster display on the very front of the theater and the striking image of Jimmy in his red jacket had a surreal look to it. The drizzle had picked up since the early morning hour and it soaked my face, in a refreshing way that is hard to describe. It was the aura of James Stark, Jimmy's character in the movie that engulfed my entire persona. I began to pout my lips and walked with a tough guy walk. The entire show was over five or six hours and as I approached Mr. Switzman's candy store it was time for an egg cream. For those of you who are wondering what an egg cream is, these are the ingredients. An egg cream has no eggs or cream in its recipe. It is a blend of milk, chocolate syrup and seltzer. As Mr. Switzman was making one for me, he was extremely interested in what new movies I saw and waiting for my review. He was an old time movie buff and never stopped talking about his grandfather. It turned out that his grandad was a bit actor and had many minor roles in some pretty impressive feature films. Abe, Mr. Switzman was extremely fond of the *King Kong* story regarding his grandfather being one of the guys who King Kong throws off

the log. Douglas Fairbanks Jr. was one of his closest friends and Abe had several photos in an album which included the aforementioned facts. As I drank my egg cream I began describing just how good the movie was, I even went so far as to say it will be in the running for best picture. Then I told of the consummate performance by James Dean, I gave him the highest praise. Abe said that even I never acted with so much excitement over any movie or it's star in the past. It can be noted that I didn't leave out Natalie Wood or Sal Mineo. Both of these actors added to the movie and they too gave memorable, flawless performances.

That following Monday when I returned to school everyone wanted a review of the new Tarzan movie. To my classmates surprise I couldn't stop talking about James Dean and even said that on Saturday I was definitely going back to see the movie again. When a star has that kind of impact on an individual like myself who was a seasoned movie critic, it's special. I had lots of hobbies, building plastic models, collecting stamps, and painting. I also played baseball, football, basketball and bowling. However, movies were my ultimate passion and I never missed my weekly double feature. The Oscar show in the Spring was an event I eagerly awaited each year. Now I had two categories I knew would win. Best picture, *Rebel Without a Cause*, and best actor, James Dean. Now more than ever I began to research Jimmy but it was a most difficult task. There was no internet to rely on, television was in its infancy and most libraries didn't stock back issues of magazines. I did have one chance of getting the scope on Jimmy regarding his previous performances. My favorite uncle, Hank who lived in Greenwich Village was a big movie buff. When I was real young he would take me to Times Square to catch the latest movies. His favorite genres were the action adventure flicks and cowboy and gangster themes were right up there on his list. As I suspected he knew quite a bit about Jimmy and even watched all of his early work on television. According to my expert uncle he had never witnessed any actor with such talent. It was an endorsement that made my evaluation of James Dean a correct one. Now I knew I had to investigate each and every available TV show he was in. It would be a very difficult task because VCR technology and the Internet were decades away. Most of the early television shows were repeated numerous times because they were quite difficult to produce. These shows were also very expensive and most if not all of the networks were in their infancy so to speak. My search for more material in the form of these teleplays was getting nowhere. The only source of printed material was the weekly edition of TV Guide. I would read the daily listings hoping to find a show with the name James Dean in the cast but kept coming up empty. Then fate kicked in. Call it luck or fate but one Sunday afternoon I was visiting an uncle outside of New York City. He lived in a small expensive suburb named Briarcliff Manor. It turned out that one of his neighbors was head of production at CBS studios in Manhattan. The gentleman was in his mid-forties and even though he was already a multi millionaire he liked my company. It was my love of sports and the movies that held his interest. After lunch we would literally spend hours discussing all the movies I had the opportunity to watch on Saturday mornings. His name was Ray and he was so busy running the CBS studio that he never had the opportunity to get to the movies. Remember this is the 1950's and if you wanted to see a movie you had to go to a movie theater. Ray was very interested in my thoughts about this new star but he had already had the good fortune to meet him when he did a show about a year ago. The one trait that stood out about Jimmy was his ability to immediately come the center of attraction. Ray went on to say that all of the production people at his company were also cognizant of that factor. The girls that worked throughout the CBS facility all acted like Frank Sinatra was in the building whenever they got word that Jimmy was on set. Then it hit both of us at almost the same time. Ray had access to all of the teleplays that had been made. Of course it wasn't videotape but the old 35mm cameras were in many ways just as good. He made arrangements for me to meet with a gentleman in charge of the movie library and the rest was up to me. It turned out that the best day of the week to begin watching the shows was Friday. The guy's name was Charlie Baker and he explained to me in a phone conversation that most of the people who worked in his department always left work shortly after lunch. Friday was the best day of the week for me also

because I was still in school and Friday was also a getaway day for some of my teachers. The very next Friday I decided to make my way to the studio around 1:00PM. The ride to CBS in Manhattan was a smooth one on the famous A train subway which was around the corner from where I lived. The only time the subway in New York was crowded was in the morning and evening rush hours. Ray had notified the front desk that I was coming and upon my arrival I was greeted with an enthusiastic welcome. Charlie, was almost like a character out of an old silent movie. He was wearing baggy pants and a vest that had a big gold chain dangling with an even bigger watch half tucked in his pocket. As he extended his hand to greet me a chill of excitement filled my body. Here I was in a TV studio with access to all the shows that James Dean was in. Charlie was a meticulous individual and his desk was more than neat. He opened a ledger and the handwriting inside was bold script, extremely clear. As he went through the list of shows each time the name James Dean appeared he wrote on a paper the code associated with it. In all there were over twenty shows. I was immediately awestruck and knew watching even half would take several weeks. Mr. Baker, "I don't think I can watch too many of the teleplays today". "Son, just call me Charlie, my boss told me to let you come back as often as you like". This was beyond my wildest expectations. I decided to watch them in chronological order and take notes for a report I decided to make. The very first one on the list was The Family Theater production of "Hill Number One." This show was a lot longer than I expected, a full hour when it first aired. When you account for the omitted commercials it was about 46 minutes in length. The vault where the teleplays were stored was as neat as Charlie's desk. Each episode was in giant color-coded movie cans. The numbering system made locating the episodes very easy. This first one was in a bright blue canister and loading the film into the projector was a breeze. The year was 1951 and this television production was aired four years before the release of the iconic *Rebel Without a Cause*. The first part of the drama was set during the Korean War. A padre addresses the company of soldiers on Easter Sunday. It is implied the army outpost is located at the base of Golgotha, the place where Jesus Christ was crucified.

The story then switches to the past, and the audience is taken back to biblical times. What makes this drama important when building a case for Jimmy receiving an Oscar begins here. The list of seasoned actors and actresses in this drama is awe inspiring. Roddy McDowell, Leif Erickson, Henry Brandon, Jeanne Cagney, Regis Toomey, Michael Ansara, Gene Lockhart, Joan Leslie, William Schallert, Nelson Leigh and Frank Wilcox. If you watch the drama Jimmy will be the one actor you remember and will most definitely stand out. Maybe it will be his few lines in the unique way he delivered them. Perhaps it will be his look, and mannerisms. Then there is the chance it will be both of these traits and more. He was only nineteen years old and holding his own against this list of veteran actors. I wanted to watch a few more shows but Charlie had some work to do at home. We left the building together and he said he looked forward to seeing me next week. The ride to my house on the subway was rather quick and when I entered my room I was certain that today was special. I have always had premonitions that on more than one occasion manifested themselves. The movies had always been a part of my life that satisfied my desires to be more than just a guy who was growing up in a big city environment. I wanted to somehow get in the movies or at least be a part of their history. The week ahead seemed to drag but by Friday I was ready to watch one or maybe a couple of the TV shows that I was more than lucky to have access to. Charlie was working on some project and he gave me the key to the vault. He was both confident and trusting that I would take care of the reels of film and the valuable equipment. It turned out that there were a lot more TV shows that James Dean had to his credit. When an individual chooses acting as his or her profession, most of the time it takes years and years before they even get minor roles. Jimmy was quite the opposite. He had worked with some of Hollywood's biggest stars on television before breaking into the movies. The networks on television were a way for actors and actresses to get valuable exposure. Jimmy worked it seemed for all of them, simultaneously. There was the General Electric Theater, Philco Television Playhouse, Campbell Summer Soundstage, Kate Smith Hour, Lux Video Television Theater, The Stu Erwin Show, Tales of

Tomorrow, The United Steel Hour, Westinghouse Studio One, Treasury Men in Action, Armstrong Circle Theater, Kraft Television Theater, Omnibus, Hallmark Hall of Fame and The Big Story. Jimmy had roles in all of these major shows and some others. It was my good fortune to have access to all of them. As the weeks went by and I watched as many as time would allow I was convinced he was unique and one of the most unusual and dynamic actors I had ever seen. The performances all stood out but there was one in particular that was so good I watched it a total of three times. The episode I am referring to was part of an anthology series. The original air date was November 11, 1953. The show was the Kraft Television Theater and it was one hour in length. Most of the early teleplays were only thirty minutes and with commercials they were a short twenty two to twenty four minutes long. The name of the episode Jimmy starred in was, A Long Time Till Dawn. To fully understand my evaluation is not at all prejudiced. You must watch it to draw your own conclusions. After my book about Errol Flynn was published, numerous people wrote to me after they followed my suggestion to watch specific movies of his. I wanted my audience to see for themselves just how good Errol was able to translate the characters he was portraying with right on excellence. The episode, A Long Time Till Dawn is an excellent starting point to use when deciding if I am correct. Of course you can also make the argument that most if not all of Jimmy's work was way above par. He had that something special that comes along once in a lifetime. A Long Time Till Dawn, will literally leave you breathless. Jimmy gives a performance that makes you compare him once again to Brando, maybe even Robert De Niro or Montgomery Cliff. It's a consummate performance. Each and every scene dripping with emotions. Visual mannerisms that have no equal. He didn't know it but he was already at the top of his game. If the argument can be made for Oscar consideration watch this teleplay. You will be more than convinced that this can be added to his body of work in the only three motion picture roles he performed.

CHAPTER 3

Only a Few People Had Television Sets

WHEN JIMMY WAS CAST in the General Electric Theater TV production of *I'm A Fool*, it was an ironic twist that one of the cast members was Natalie Wood. The original air date was November 14, 1954 and most families didn't own a television set. The ones that did told all of their friends about the handsome young actor who was the star of this very early teleplay. It was a unique story narrated by Eddie Albert who was the older version of the James Dean character. This was the age of "live" TV with no second takes. If an actor flubbed his lines, that is what the audience got. It can be noted that most if not all of the reviews regarding this teleplay are very negative. The reviews describe the entire production as amateurish, the story is not interesting and James Dean's performance rather forgettable. If you have not

seen this teleplay by all means please seek it out and you can judge for yourself whether or not the description you are about to read is accurate.

The story is about a young man portrayed by Jimmy who decides it's time for him to leave his home and family and begin his life as an adult while finding a job. He ends up at a racetrack and meets a stablemate who at first belittles him but then they become good friends. One day as they are traveling in a wagon there is a chance meeting with a beautiful young girl portrayed by Natalie Wood. It is a very short scene, but the chemistry between Jimmy and Natalie would manifest itself in the very near future, when in a twist of fate in both of their careers they were cast in the classic *Rebel Without a Cause*. In the next scene Natalie's character is spending a day at the race track with her brother and a friend when they encounter Jimmy near the grandstand. In his effort to impress Natalie he spins a tale about coming from a very wealthy family. The race horse in the next race is owned by his dad, and the lies about who he is and where his family is from get bigger and bigger. In the end the two potential lovers part and it is evident they will never see each other again. It would be very hard for you to understand just how great an actor Jimmy was even in this very early role if you only watch it one time. The main problem that I see with the negative reviews regarding his performance deal with the entire production. The studios were limited by budget restraints in the early 1950's and all of these "live" teleplays were in many ways experimental. They were the foundation of what this brand new media of television would eventually evolve into. This particular episode featured actual cardboard sets and even had a screen with a motion picture running behind the wagon scene in order to depict the illusion of the two actors riding in an open wagon as the landscape passes by. Jimmy made the most of his character and his way with words which later in his short career became a sort of trademark added to the drama. His movements and complete body language were already vintage Dean. In the scene at the racetrack he was wearing a foolish outfit complete with a hat and it might have been a complete disaster if not for his unique persona. The audience had to be driven in by the way he handled the entire situation. As was stated previously, it might not be evident by your

first viewing but after the second you will certainly agree. One of the players in this early teleplay was veteran character actor Roy Glenn. He was the first person Jimmy came into contact with at the racing stable and it can be debated that Jimmy held his own in this scene with the veteran Glenn. In the final scene where he kisses Natalie goodbye, his facial expressions, as well as, his demeanor are spot on.

When The Unlighted Road, another early teleplay aired on television in May of 1953, James Dean was already without him knowing it becoming a "teen idol". The short story was even introduced by Jimmy who described the very unique play while sitting in a small setting. Here is the opening description exactly as it appeared on television in Jimmy's own words. This play is the story of a young man named Jeffery Latham, who opened the door of a very ordinary, innocent-looking roadside diner, and he saw his whole life change. Jimmy's character, Jeffrey Latham is a restless young man from Wisconsin, who has just ended his stint in Korea. With little luck hitchhiking after dark, Jeffrey enters the diner, and orders coffee and a sandwich. While finishing the meal he goes behind the counter to fix proprietor Murvyn Vye's broken coffee pot, thus revealing he's worked in diners. Mr. Vye needs help in the coffee shop, and offers Dean a job, and a room. Jimmy hesitates but then decides he might as well accept the offer and the drama is set. Veteran character actor Mike Deegan plays Murvyn Vye. In the next scene when you watch Jimmy, try to examine all of his mannerisms even his voice and facial movements. It is a certainty that the comparison between Jimmy and Marlon Brando will take you by complete surprise. This small detail is very important in developing a case for Jimmy to receive an Oscar because these early examples of his ability to not only capture a scene but engulf the audience are truly remarkable. There have only been a small handful of actors or actresses that can make that claim. Jimmy was the one that was able to do it on numerous occasions, if not in every performance he ever gave. As the half hour show progresses it is quite evident that Jimmy looks like he is in complete control of all of the situations that follow. He interacts with a girl he meets played by Pat Hardy, who was a real-life friend of Jimmy. The bond

between the two that developed is all created by his mannerisms. If you have the opportunity to view his episode before viewing *Rebel Without a Cause*, it is guaranteed that you will definitely see the comparison between both of those roles as almost identical. It can be noted that this teleplay was made after Jimmy starred in his first movie, *East of Eden*. Today that would be a very rare occasion that an actor would go from his big screen motion picture debut then back to the small screen in the same year. One of the reasons why Jimmy took these television roles was because of his determination to be a great movie star. For some strange reason he knew deep inside that his destiny was acting, and he made sure he would act every chance he got no matter what the medium was.

Appearing after the premiere of "*East of Eden*", this short drama was no great shakes, relatively speaking. Still, "The Unlighted Road" is a neat little play. Writer Walter C. Brown, Dean, and the cast perform admirably. With Brown's script, Dean is able create a sympathetic character. And, it's nice to see Dean, newly a big screen "movie star", still appearing in an occasional small screen drama.

CHAPTER 4

If You Could Return
to the 1950's

THE DECADE OF THE 1950's was one that produced some of the greatest motion pictures of all time. One year during that decade stands out, 1955, and the movie *Rebel Without a Cause* released in 1955, is the movie that most people associate with James Dean. In 1955, the Oscar nominations for best actor and their respective movies were the following: Marlon Brando, *On the Waterfront*, Humphrey Bogart, *The Caine Mutiny*, Bing Crosby, *The Country Girl*, James Mason, *A Star Is Born*, and Dan O'Herlihy in *The Adventures of Robinson Crusoe*. The winner was Marlon Brando. There is no question that Marlon was deserving of the Oscar but what about James Dean's truly unforgettable performance in *Rebel Without a Cause*? The fact that Jimmy made only three motion pictures and two of them did receive Oscar

WARNER BROS. ST
WARDROBE TES
FOR
#403 GIANT
OF
JAMES DEA
AS
JETT
WARDROBE CHANGE # 8
WORN IN { SET EXT HIGHW
SCENE 277
W·B   55

nominations is quite puzzling. When you evaluate the three performances by the order of their respective value in determining Oscar worthy quality there is a major contradiction. The reason why the term contradiction is used deals with where those three James Dean movies rank in motion picture history. As a matter of fact when the American Film Institute compiled numerous lists regarding every aspect of the movie and television media James Dean and his three movies are all high on their respective categories. For example AFI's 50 Greatest American Screen Legends has Jimmy at number 18. He is sandwiched between Kirk Douglas at 17 and Burt Lancaster at 19. Those two movie actors were unique and memorable for their outstanding roles and made many great movies together. On the list of AFI's 100 Greatest American Movies Of All Time the contradiction can be made due to the fact of where two of Jimmy's movies rank. *Giant* is listed at 82, while *Rebel Without a Cause* was placed at 59. It can be noted that number 60 was *Raiders of The Lost Ark* and number 61 was *Vertigo*. When the nominations for best picture were made *Giant* did get a nomination but *Rebel Without a Cause* did not. It is evident that a gap of 23 places on the American Film Institute's list of the 100 Greatest American Movies Of All Time is a very substantial one. It makes the argument more credible that the performances turned in by Jimmy in all three of his movies deserved equal Oscar nomination consideration. The difference between those two performances, *Giant* and *Rebel Without a Cause* is in some instances too close to call. When Jimmy approached the role of James Stark in *Rebel Without a Cause*, right in the very first scene he improvised. The audience was mesmerized by his unique and unconventional style of acting. Jimmy was just being Jimmy but it came across magnificently. He stole the show so to speak. After watching that opening scene in the police station numerous times it really gets better and better. It is so believable you feel like your right there with him. Each and every emotion coming out of the character moves you like only a very few performances ever did in the past. Some of the other qualities that were present in the entire performance can only be described as brilliant. The supporting cast were all Hollywood heavyweights. Jim Backus and Ann Doran could not have been any better

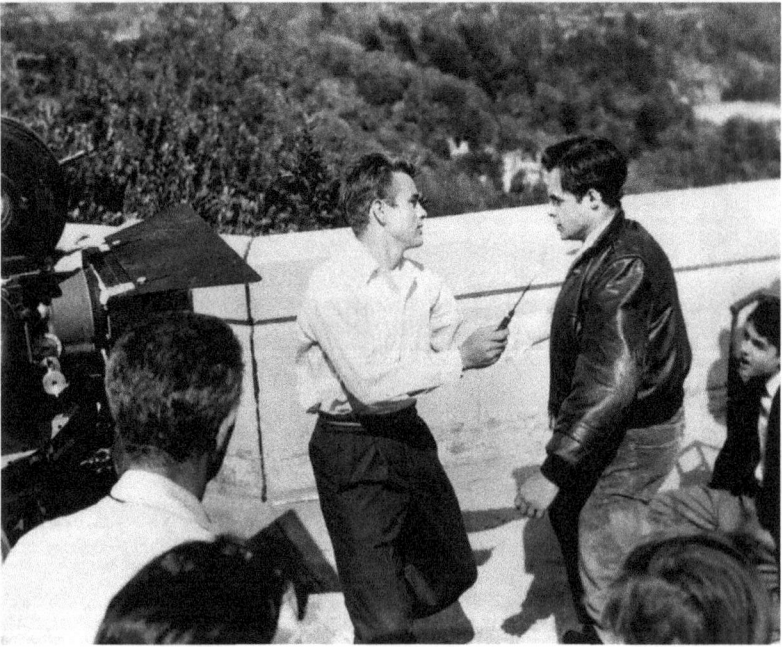

as the parents of Jimmy. Whenever they were in a scene together with Jimmy, the interaction was always right on the mark. It was like watching your own family and the similar struggles you might have encountered. There is also a scene at the beginning of the movie that unless you watch it multiple times the realism and sensitivity Jimmy displays might not come through. It is Jimmy meeting Natalie Wood for the second time, the first was a very brief encounter at the police station. As this scene begins Jimmy is ready for his first day at his new school. He is gazing out his kitchen window and as he parts the curtain he spots Natalie leaving her house. Jimmy's mom and dad are sitting at the kitchen table and they are both treating him like a small child. It is here where the greatness of Dean begins to shine through and take hold of the audience. His movements and body language is unequaled in comparison to other actors. Jimmy's interaction with his mom and dad's statements are mostly met with gestures. He speaks only a few words but his expressions are far more compelling. The scene switches to the side of his house and Natalie is walking near the front. We don't see Jimmy but he calls out and then he jumps up behind a big white picket fence. I am convinced that jumping gesture was completely improvised by him and is what made this interaction with Natalie so special. In the annals of motion picture couples, Natalie Wood and James Dean should be included when Hollywood speaks of their greatest screen legend couples. It would not be inconceivable to visualize both of them playing in several other movies together if fate had not dealt Jimmy his tragic fate. Getting back to the scene, Jimmy catches up to Natalie and the chemistry as she acts distant from his obvious interest in her. The background music is as compelling as the scene itself and he glides along as if time and space is irrelevant. Now the scene takes hold as Natalie asks, "you wanna carry my books?" His reply was, "I got my car, wanna go with me?" She replies "I go with the kids." During this entire dialog they both are gazing into each other's eyes and Jimmy was able to convince everyone he was smitten. It was not his words but his mannerisms and facial gestures that told exactly what was on his mind. We were treated to an amazing bit of acting from not only Jimmy but also Natalie who was already a seasoned actress, and

only seventeen years of age. As a testimony of her greatness when the Oscar nominations for 1955 were given, Natalie received a best supporting actress nomination for this role. It should be noted that Natalie was nominated two more times in the best actress category. The first was for her great performance in *Splendor in the Grass*, and then for *Love with the Proper Stranger*. Even though *Rebel Without a Cause* failed to get Jimmy an Oscar nomination he most likely turned in his best performance without knowing it.

As the movie progressed the character of James Stark was so compelling and memorable that some sixty years later it stands alone as a one of a kind performance. It has to be compared with some of the other great characters of all time. Don Vito Corleone, the character Marlon Brando brought so vividly to life in *The Godfather*. Clint Eastwood's, detective Harry Callahan in the *Dirty Harry* movies. Then there was Humphrey Bogart as Rick Blaine in *Casablanca* and as Fred C. Dobbs in *The Treasure of the Sierra Madre*. All of these characters stand out because they had a uniqueness and level of perfection that is seldom achieved. James Stark would have been just another rebellious youth if it was not for the over the top performance James Dean gave. He actually evoked every possible trait that James Stark would have had if he was a real person. However for the entire one hour and fifty-one minutes that featured Jimmy, there he was as real as could be. James Stark came to life and became a life like breathing human being right before your eyes. The movie, *Rebel Without a Cause*, had excellent individuals behind the camera. It was directed by Nicholas Ray who mastered the art of color in his productions. The producer was David Weisbart. *Rebel Without a Cause* also had one of the greatest cinematographers of all time Ernest Haller on board. He was nominated seven times for best cinematography and won for *Gone With The Wind*. The music was produced by another two time Oscar winner Leonard Rosenman. The unusual fact that all these Hollywood greats have in common is they all worked with James Dean in *Rebel Without a Cause*. Many of the movies most memorable moments are how these men used their trades to enhance the production. The use of outdoor scenery and locations rather than sound stages was important to all of them. Jimmy

enjoyed working with this illustrious group of filmmakers. On the other hand they enjoyed working with his improvised way of acting. They never knew what to expect from Jimmy each and every day, he was very unpredictable. The melding of all of these qualities made the movie an instant classic. A good example is one of the many scenes which everyone associates with the movie, a scene played out at the Griffith Park Observatory in Los Angeles. However before we evaluate Jimmy's performance in this scene an important cast member must be introduced. During Jimmy's first day at school he had a chance meeting with the character, Plato aptly played by Sal Mineo. Right from the very first encounter at the police station until this character development scene, they were magnetic together. Sal Mineo was no lightweight and he and Jimmy would both create a memorable screen relationship. Plato, was an innocent youth and he visualized Jim Stark as a much needed father figure. Mineo did such a good job with his portrayal that he received an Oscar nomination for best supporting actor. The Oscar ultimately went to another Hollywood great, Jack Lemmon for *Mister Roberts*. This is just another example of how too many factors are utilized when both the nominations and the winners are decided for Oscar consideration. It would not be fair to take away the outstanding work Sal Mineo did in *Rebel Without a Cause*. However it was unfair that both actors did not receive the nomination. The case can be made relative to their performances in this great movie that they definitely were equally deserving of the prestigious nominations. The Griffith Park Observatory scene has over the years taken on a life of its own. There have been over thirty more movies and at least that many television shows which used this location but Rebel Without a Cause is the one most associated with the park. It can also be noted that two scenes were shot at the park for «Rebel», one inside the planetarium, the other outside. A monument with a bust of James Dean is located where you can take a photo and also get the iconic Hollywood Sign in the same frame. An identical monument has been placed at the James Dean Memorial Park in Fairmount, Indiana, the hometown of Jimmy.

When the scene was shot the weather was perfect, a bright sunny

California sky as a backdrop. James Dean and Sal Mineo were talking in an area overlooking one of the many observation decks. Jimmy had parked his car just below where they were and a large group of teenagers was approaching the car from an adjacent ramp. The leader of the group noticed Jimmy and Plato, Sal Mineo's character and the action was about to begin. Natalie Wood was one of the girls and in this gang there were many Hollywood future stars.

There was a relatively unknown actor at the time, Corey Allen who played Buzz, the gangs leader. Dennis Hopper and Nick Adams were also part of the gang. When the group of tough guys and girls looked up at Jimmy and Plato, Buzz walked over to Jimmy's car. He took out a switchblade and teased Jimmy by stroking his white wall tire. Then he punctured the tire. Jimmy came down the walk way and casually opened the trunk of his car, took out his jack and stated "you know something, you read too many comic books". The entire audience was expecting Jimmy to explode, waiting for the inevitable confrontation. The confrontation was halted temporarily by Jimmy's coolness. Shortly thereafter Buzz says the word chicken and it infuriates Jimmy and the action heats up to a crescendo. A famous knife fight takes place and this is why it is so important to the case for an Oscar. The entire scene was highlighted with a fantastic soundtrack that enhanced the action and drama. From the time Jimmy watched the group and the puncturing of his tire, he used very little dialogue. His total domination over all of the other male stars was unique. Even though all of the males in the gang including Buzz were delinquent types Jimmy's look was much different. The guys had the 1950's tough guy haircuts and clothes. Jimmy had his tough guy haircut, more like an Elvis look. Even though he wore a suit and white shirt he stood out, in each and every way. He used sighs to his advantage. He tilted his head and shrugged his shoulders in unison. Most actors when given the opportunity to play a similar part over act. They most likely would have yelled at Buzz, pulled some kind of tantrum. The scene would just be a solo guy who had no chance of capturing the audience. Jimmy, on the contrary, held the audience in the palm of his hand. It was Jim Stark they were watching on the screen. The movie was just beginning to develop a plot and storyline and it was dynamic mainly because all the elements that make a movie a

classic one were in place. James Dean was without him knowing it about to change an entire generation. The change would be so dominant that some sixty plus years later it still has a lasting effect on everyone who watches it. In the history of memorable movie scenes and characters this scene stands alone, Jim Stark the character Jimmy created is unforgettable and immortal. Most of the little special touches were all improvised by Jimmy. There are many memorable moments in the movie. Some of these moments and scenes are the things that make audiences return over and over to the movies. Another scene that captivated audiences was the one that took place soon after the Griffith Observatory one. It was shot at night and that factor added to the atmosphere, a cutting edge. The scene was filmed in Calabasas, California on a cliff overlooking the Pacific Ocean. It was the culmination of a dare given to Jimmy from Buzz after the knife fight. The two boys agree to do the "chickie run", or a chicken race, wherein they test their gall and bravery by driving stolen cars to a cliff and racing them toward the edge. The first person to jump out of their vehicle is a chicken. This was another highlight of James Dean's outstanding interpretation and improvised acting skills. It is also a good place to remind the audience that James Dean was not the original actor who was chosen to play Jim Stark. In one of the many twists of fate associated with the movie and James Dean it was actually Marlon Brando who was to play Jim Stark. These two actors have always been compared to each other, almost as if they were brothers. Before the actual chicken run, Buzz and Jimmy exchange pleasantries. The dialog between the two rivals was rather ironic. Buzz: I like you, you know? Jim: Buzz? What are we doing this for? Buzz: (still quiet) We got to do something. Don't we? Leading up to when the cars motors rev up and the race is about to begin, Buzz interacts with Judy, Natalie Wood's character by asking her for some dirt. As he rubs his hands together Jim glances in their direction and calls Judy. He looks at her with a cute smile, he too asked for some dirt. Two very important points must be made regarding this scene and just how good a performance Jimmy turned in. First, the cinematography with the illumination of the cars lights on each side of where the race was to take place was perfect. The camera angles most definitely

added to the overall drama. One camera was shooting from ground level, it captured the two cars as they drove past Natalie. Second, Jimmy completely dominated a scene where one of the lead characters was about to crash his car over a cliff and perish. He managed to invoke a complete air of boyish innocence. With all the danger and drama around him he was able to convey a devil may care attitude, all the while controlling the entire scene. Once again James Dean was without knowing it making cinematic history. He even wore his iconic red jacket for this scene. That jacket has become synonymous with the aura surrounding James Dean. Then at the culmination of the scene, after everyone looked below the cliff where Buzz crashed Jimmy made another iconic gesture. As Natalie stood frozen with grief. Her eyes mesmerized at the water below crashing on the rocks. Jimmy slowly reaches out his hand, never moving from his spot and when their fingers touched and eyes met it was all James Dean. His red jacket glistening from the moon beams. Later in the movie Jimmy and Natalie created a most memorable love scene. Keep in mind Natalie was still a teenager in real life. This was her very first love scene. The two young actors were lying fully clothed and Natalie told Jimmy she loved him. Jimmy radiated that feeling without any movement. It was his eyes and unique gestures that gave Natalie the answer she wanted. The two young lovers kissed. It was not a passionate kiss. This innocent kiss conveyed the love the two were hoping to find. A very touching and heart-rendering moment in cinematic history.

Rebel Without a Cause was released on October 27, 1955. It was a Thursday, almost a month earlier on September 30, 1955, a Friday, Jimmy met his fate. The important things that made life special during that era have stayed with us forever. Many classic movies were also released during that period of time. Humphrey Bogart starred in *The Desperate Hours*, Gordon MacRae sang in *Oklahoma!* In an ironic note both Marlon Brando and Frank Sinatra starred in *Guys and Dolls*. Jimmy has often been compared to both of these Oscar winning actors. The great drama *Picnic*, with William Holden and Kim Novak captivated audiences. It was a special time for movies and the top songs were all timeless hits. Rock and Roll was just heating up with

Bill Haley's, Rock Around The Clock hit. Fess Parker as Davy Crockett was one of television's biggest shows. The performance by Jimmy was overlooked when it came to awards and recognition. Even the movie was missing from all the nominations. It is extremely difficult to try to explain the following details regarding how various award committees reacted to the movie and James Dean. The movie did not get nominated by the Academy for the best picture Oscar. There were three Oscar nominations, both Natalie Wood and Sal Mineo were nominated for their best supporting roles. Nicholas Ray was nominated for the best writing Oscar. All three lost. The best supporting actor Oscar went to Jack Lemmon for *Mister Roberts*. In the best supporting actress category Jo Van Fleet won for her role in *East of Eden*. The best writing Oscar went to Daniel Fuchs for *Love Me Or Leave Me*. The only award that *Rebel Without a Cause* won was a Golden Globe to Natalie Wood for best newcomer. When you think of James Dean, you picture him in the red jacket he wore in *Rebel Without a Cause*. It is a thought provoking image that everyone who has even the smallest interest in Jimmy associates with him. It would be very difficult to come up with a handful of actors in the entire last century that possessed that quality. The character of James Stark that Jimmy created most definitely changed an entire generation of young men. That generation of young men was not limited to those in the United States but the entire world. An ironic twist regarding the movie and it characters, especially Jimmy is as follows. One of the stars, Sal Mineo dies near the last scene of the movie. However the director had a very different ending in mind. Nicholas Ray, the director wanted to use an alternative ending. He actually filmed that alternate ending to *Rebel Without a Cause* where Jim Stark, Jimmy's character is shot and killed by the police. We will never know why he decided to use the one where Sal Mineo is shot instead, ironic fact. There is only one more movie to discuss that Jimmy made. The movie was *Giant*. It was a movie with some of the greatest actors that ever graced the big screen. James Dean was one of those movie giants and he was as big as the movie's title. He was a star but this would be the final act in one of Hollywood's most iconic male actor's life.

CHAPTER 5

Errol, Marilyn and Jimmy

"Everybody says I can't act. They said the same thing about Elizabeth Taylor. And they were wrong. She was great in A Place in the Sun. I'll never get the right part, anything I really want. My looks are against me. They're too specific."
- Marilyn

"It isn't what they say about you, it's what they whisper." - Errol

"To my way of thinking, an actor's course is set even before he's out of the cradle."
– Jimmy

IT CAN BE SAID THAT the great swashbuckling hero, Errol Flynn had a female counterpart, Marilyn Monroe. The main reason for this comparison is based on several unique characteristics that these two iconic movie stars shared. First and foremost was there voracious desire to be with the opposite sex. Both were linked with literally hundreds of romantic partners throughout their short but interesting careers. It can also be noted that strange as it seems they were both married three times, but all of the marriages never lasted. One can only wonder what kind of relationship Marilyn Monroe would have had with Errol Flynn? The second characteristic that they both shared dealt with how the two approached their careers as actors in Hollywood's Golden Age. It was a special time when the stars were always much bigger and important then the movies they starred in. Your average movie patron was attracted to the stars of the movie that he or she decided to attend. If you make a comparison between all of the movies that both Errol Flynn and Marilyn Monroe starred in with most of the movies released today there are also very unique differences. The movies of today rely on special effects and big budgets, coupled with millions of dollars in promotion. These current releases seldom rely on a complex script and are really not entertaining. The performances that the stars of today are convoluted and contrived. If you evaluate the majority of the movies that Errol Flynn and Marilyn Monroe were in, almost all had a dynamic script and the only promotion the movies had were trailers in the theaters and print advertisements. Looking at the cost of promotion in the Golden Age of Hollywood as compared to today the difference is in the tens of millions. Most of the movies that would not be considered as blockbuster movies by today's standards always were box office hits because of who starred in them and the complexity of the script. These movies could be about virtually any subject, any genre but they had "stars" in the cast. Today the movies that 90% of the time make the top ten list at the box office each weekend most likely have some sort of CGI in their subject matter, and they are productions that are finished in a matter of weeks. In the days when a western made its debut, you could find such big names such as Errol Flynn, Bogart, Cagney, Quinn and Heston in the cast. The western would most likely be a drama that relied heavily on its story and characters. They were always entertaining. That level of entertainment came from the presence of the big name stars who were in the cast. Errol Flynn made a lot of these movies and from a box office standpoint they were always very successful because of the name Errol Flynn in the cast. The same can be said of Marilyn, she was an instant box office draw. When the movies that Marilyn Monroe and Errol Flynn were being produced the way they approached their job, if you want to

call it a job, was a mirror image. Errol Flynn on numerous occasions would decide he wanted to sail the Caribbean in one of his yachts. The problem with his decision was he made the choice while he was in the very middle of starring in a movie. The 1950's were light years away from the internet, cell phones and there was virtually no way to reach anyone who was somewhere docked off shore in a tropical paradise. To make matters worse for Errol Flynn's studio, Warner Brothers, when he returned to the site of the film shoot Errol Flynn would go right back on his yacht. He probably didn't plan it that way but he was a free spirit. If he felt the admonishment from one of the Warner Brothers was too harsh, he would not argue, with the Warner in question. Errol would simply smile and give a wave of his hand and off he was, again. It was not unusual for one of Errol Flynn's productions to be shut down for months and not days because of his seafaring ways, a cavalier attitude. Marilyn Monroe didn't have any yacht to take her away from a movie set, Marilyn decided on her own terms what being late was all about. When Marilyn first entered the movie business she was always very dependable, always on time for set rehearsals, and studied her lines meticulously. True in the early part of her movie career those lines were few and far between, buy she was extremely dedicated and a perfectionist. In some cases Marilyn was merely a walk on, but made sure that walk on part would be noticed. The bigger Marilyn's star power grew the more her habit of being late on the set or not showing up at all most likely infuriated the producers and directors she was working with immensely. This habit contributed to the fact that when it was time for the ballots to be cast for an Academy Award, Marilyn Monroe's name was always omitted, as was the case in Errol Flynn. One of the most famous confirmations of the fact that everyone connected to the production of a movie in Hollywood knew how widespread Marilyn's lateness was, surfaced at a most prominent place. The event was in New York City at Madison Square Garden, it was a birthday celebration for the then President of the United States, John F. Kennedy. Peter Lawford was the master of ceremonies and as Marilyn Monroe made her way to the microphone to sing happy birthday to the President, Mr. Lawford introduced her as "the late Marilyn Monroe." There were many more similarities but another hard to debate trait that both Errol Flynn and Marilyn Monroe shared was there on screen presence. Of course during the era when they were making movies Hollywood was full of many glamorous movie actresses and handsome leading men. The differences that set the both of them apart from all of the others was a unique and electrifying persona that seemed to jump at you from the screen. It didn't matter what role either of them was cast in or who was their co-star, Errol Flynn and Marilyn Monroe both literally lit up the screen. That quality that they both possessed was present in both of their careers the very first time you saw them, the very first time. The following list of movies that they are famous for, movies that are on everyone's list of the greatest of all time. These movies are just a sampling of some of the two stars best and memorable performances. First, we have Marilyn's Oscar worthy performance that should have at least been nominated. *Some Like it Hot*, how did she get overlooked. The movie is considered the best comedy of all time. Then in *The Seven Year Itch*, she turned in a performance that was before its time. Marilyn was what made the movie a classic, and she was listed in the credits as The Girl. The skirt scene in The *Seven Year Itch* is Hollywood's number one memorable scene of all time. The image of Marilyn, the skirt blowing in the wind has even been immortalized by a 36 foot steel statue. *The Misfits*, a movie that showed how Marilyn could play opposite Hollywood's biggest male star, Clark Gable and equal him with her performance. *Gentlemen Prefer Blondes*, she could dance, she could act she could sing. Her "Diamonds are a Girl's Best Friend" rendition in that movie is one that everyone remembers. *Bus Stop*, a great dramatic performance with songs included. In addition some memorable minor and not so minor roles that formulated her style of acting. That list of movies includes *All About Eve*, *The Asphalt Jungle*, *Niagara*, and even *The River of No Return*. As far as Errol Flynn goes, *The Adventures of Robin Hood*, is the greatest action adventure movie of all time. A bold statement but Errol was able to create a Robin Hood that was pure perfection. The way he talked, the way he fought, the way he made you believe you were watching Robin Hood.. His pirate sagas are unequaled in the characters he

Errol Flynn

Warner Bros.

portrayed. *Captain Blood*, made him an instant Hollywood idol, his very first starring role. Then his role in *The Sea Hawk* most likely is responsible for getting him named the number one movie pirate of all time. He even beat out Captain Jack Sparrow to get that honor. In *They Died With Their Boots On*, Errol's portrayal of Custer will not only bring you excitement but in one memorable scene, to tears. He proved he could play any historical character with believability. In *Gentlemen Jim*, Errol became Jim Corbett right before your eyes. He was the classic hero in *The Charge of the Light Brigade*. Even at the end of his short career, Errol gave what everyone thought was another award winning performance. This time In *The Sun Also Rises*, a movie that allowed Errol to play a character that was close to what he had become. In between Errol made many memorable cowboy movies, such as *Rocky Mountain, Montana, Virginia City, San Antonio, Silver River, Santa Fe Trail* and *Dodge City*. Some of the war movies that Errol starred in were, *Dive Bomber, The Dawn Patrol, Edge of Darkness*, and *Northern Pursuit*. If you have seen any of these movies you already know that Errol like Marilyn has been overlooked for his contribution to Hollywood. It really didn't matter what role they had, they made you feel you had witnessed something special. Each star in their own right has remained a timeless reminder of some day or night you spent watching them in amazement. They both truly left you the viewer with something unique, so unique that you wanted to see them again, you had to see them again. They had a magical quality that has never been duplicated, a quality that has withstood the test of time and is alluring to the audience today just as it was over fifty or sixty years ago. It is just a mere evaluation but when you are universally thought of in the manner of being iconic while you are still alive. Alive and making movies a slight air of jealousy might have accounted for neither star getting recognized for their on screen accomplishments.. Both Errol Flynn and Marilyn Monroe had their share of off screen scandals and most certainly it too played a most important role in the fact that Hollywood choose to always omit their names when the Academy Awards were being nominated. They were truly the most beautiful and interesting Hollywood actors of all time, who could act, love and live life to the fullest. Marilyn Monroe and Errol Flynn....it is beauty that captures your attention, but personality that captures your heart.

The following is a special tribute that was made about Errol Flynn after he died. It was made by a man who was one of Hollywood's most influential studio heads of all time. The statement of course was meant to describe Errol Flynn, but it is evident it can be used to describe his female counterpart, Marilyn Monroe also.

Jack L. Warner, head of the iconic Warner Brothers studios, on remembering Errol, Jack said it best, "Let's remember him for the good years! When you see a meteor stab the sky, or a bomb explode, or a fire sweep across a dry hillside, the picture is vivid and remains in your mind. So it was with Errol.... he was all the heroes in one magnificent, sexy, animal package....he showered an audience with sparks when he laughed, when he fought, or when he loved. I just wish we had someone around today half as good as Flynn."

Then we have the third great overlooked star, James Dean. Just like Marilyn Monroe and Errol Flynn, James Dean never received the most coveted of all awards given to those who choose the acting profession, The Oscar. Who in today's current group of male movie stars could possibly star in only three movies and be revered for all time? The answer is simply there is none. However, James Dean is the one and only star of all time who can lay claim to that unique fact. Hollywood is a place where dreams are made and hearts are broken. Jimmy found that his dreams did in fact become reality. Unfortunately he only got a small taste of the tremendous star he had become. He found that once in a lifetime special soul mate. A love for the ages but his heart was broken almost as fast as it was beating with love. Three unbelievable movies brought him to our hearts. Each one more memorable than its predecessor. First came *East of Eden*, then *Rebel Without a Cause and* finally *Giant*. Marilyn, Errol and Jimmy would share what is now the quest for an Oscar.

CHAPTER 6

Quotes... Another Time... Another Sandy Beach Awaits...

THIS CHAPTER NEEDS some clarification. When I began writing it the purpose was to share James Dean's quotes with his fans. However as you will see the exercise took on a life of its own. The more I selected famous people to quote, the more interesting their quotes became. I hope you enjoy sharing the wisdom and profound statements as much as I did uncovering them. Perhaps you will not only find them interesting but more than that an enlightened experience. I will even go so far as to predict some may bring a tear to your eye, but that's a good thing.

The following quotes from James Dean are quotes directly attributed to Jimmy and his memory. Most of the quotes are from James Dean, however over the years some were not made by him but will always be associated

73

with Jimmy. Before we look at Jimmy's quotes there are some quotes uttered by famous celebrities and iconic figures that should also be remembered.

Errol Flynn -

"My dream of happiness: a quiet spot by the Jamaican seashore . . . hearing the wind sob with the beauty and the tragedy of everything. Sitting under an almond tree, with the leaf spread over me like an umbrella."

Olivia De Havilland -

"I had a very big crush on Errol Flynn during 'Captain Blood.' I thought he was absolutely smashing for three solid years, but he never guessed. Then he had one on me but nothing came of it. I'm not going to regret that; it could have ruined my life."

Greer Garson -

"While Errol Flynn will be remembered by movie fans as the handsome, confident cavalier, the romantic conqueror in boudoir and battlefield, his friends and companions also will remember facets totally at variance with the heroic illusion. But they will remember, too, his wit and charm, his lifelong love of ocean and sailing ships, his fascination with sagas of buccaneers and soldiers of fortune, and his desire to live life fully as a daring adventurer - and these were characteristics which reconciled the man and the image."

Marilyn Monroe -

"Hollywood is a place where they'll pay you a thousand dollars for a kiss and fifty cents for your soul."

Veronica Lake -

"I've reached a point in my life where it's the little things that matter... I was always a rebel and probably could have got much farther had I changed my attitude. But when you think about it, I got pretty far without changing attitudes. I'm happier with that."

Fay Wray -

"When it was over my daughter said, 'Oh, I felt so sorry for him - he didn't want to hurt you, he liked you.' That was Victoria. When you visualize him up there on top of the Empire State Building, you do feel sorry for him"

Marlon Brando -

"When I lie on the beach there naked, which I do sometimes, and I feel the wind coming over me and I see the stars up above and I am looking into this very deep, indescribable night, it is something that escapes my vocabulary to describe. Then I think: 'God, I have no importance. Whatever I do or don't do, or what anybody does, is not more important than the grains of sand that I am lying on, or the coconut that I am using for my pillow.' So I really don't think in the long sense."

Charles Bronson -

"I guess I look like a rock quarry that someone has dynamited."

Laurence Olivier -

"Living is strife and torment, disappointment and love and sacrifice, golden sunsets and black storms. I said that some time ago, and today I do not think I would add one word."

Cary Grant -

"When people tell you how young you look, they are telling you how old you are."

Klaus Kinski -

"The truth is, I can never die. For I will be in everything and see you in everything and watch over you. I am your reaction in the water of a mountain lake."

John Huston -

"The directing of a picture involves coming out of your individual loneliness and taking a controlling part in putting together a small world. A picture is made. You put a frame around it and move on. And one day you die. That is all there is to it."

Walter Huston -

"Many years ago... many, many years ago, I brought up a boy, and I said to him, 'Son, if you ever become a writer, try to write a good part for your old man sometime.' Well, by cracky, that's what he did!"

James Cagney -

"You dirty, double-crossing rat."

Montgomery Clift -

"Look, I'm not odd. I'm just trying to be an actor; not a movie star, an actor."

Ernest Borgnine -

"Fathers and mothers are just people, which means they make mistakes. Don't hold that against them. Whatever flaws they may have, they created you in a moment of love, and are among the few who knew you when. When they're gone, there won't be anyone to take their place."

Burt Lancaster -

"They were fun days, and we set the town on fire with every movie we did."

Judy Garland -

"I've always taken 'The Wizard of Oz' very seriously, you know. I believe in the idea of the rainbow. And I've spent my entire life trying to get over it."

Gregory Peck -

"Inside of all the makeup and the character and makeup, it's you, and I think that's what the audience is really interested in... you, how you're going to cope with the situation, the obstacles, the troubles that the writer put in front of you."

Audie Murphy -

"I was scared before every battle. That old instinct of self-preservation is a pretty basic thing, but while the action was going on some part of my mind shut off and my training and discipline took over. I did what I had to do."

Kirk Douglas -

"Fame is as much about luck as it is about talent, perhaps more."

Victor Mclaglen -

"I have no illusions about acting and certainly I have none about myself. Long ago I came to the conclusion that actors are victims of luck and circumstance. If the role you are in fits the size of your head and some inherent quality in yourself, you do it well."

Natalie Wood -

"At night, when the sky is full of stars and the sea is still you get the wonderful sensation that you are floating in space."

Clark Gable -

"Everything Marilyn does is different from any other woman, strange and exciting, from the way she talks to the way she uses that magnificent torso."

James Coburn -

"Personality. Gotta have some kind of personality and you don't wear your personality on your body. It's gotta come from someplace."

Tony Curtis -

"I want the public to know that it will be an honor for me to meet them and spend a few special moments with all those who helped me through my filmed career."

Johnny Carson -

"Never continue in a job you don't enjoy. If you're happy in what you're doing, you'll like yourself, you'll have inner peace. And if you have that, along with physical health, you will have had more success than you could possibly have imagined."

Mickey Rooney -

"You've got to recognize, there will never be another you. It has nothing to do with ego; it happens to be the truth. There will never be another person the same. There'll never be another you."

Clint Eastwood -

"Respect your efforts, respect yourself. Self-respect leads to self-discipline. When you have both firmly under your belt, that's real power."

Scott Eastwood -

"My father's definitely old school and he raised me with integrity - to be places on time, show up and work hard."

Lionel Barrymore -

"I've got a lot of ham in me."

Roy Rogers -

"The world changed. Hollywood changed. I think we've lost something, and we don't know how to get it back."

Lee Marvin -

"As soon as people see my face on a movie screen, they knew two things: first, I'm not going to get the girl, and second, I'll get a cheap funeral before the picture is over."

Walter Brennan -

"I'm not a glamour boy, and I never get the girl. I like to play old people, because there's something to them. Did you ever see anybody under 30 with any real character or expression in his face?"

Hank Williams -

"You got to have smelt a lot of mule manure before you can sing like a hillbilly."

Robert Stack -

"In the Belgian air force a general supposedly saw a UFO, tracked it with his plane, photographed it with his wing cameras. And I believe it because I said to myself why would this person, not getting paid for this, do it unless it actually happened or he thought it did."

Orson Welles -

"Good evening, ladies and gentleman. My name is Orson Welles. I am an actor. I am a writer. I am a producer. I am a director. I am a magician. I appear onstage and on the radio. Why are there so many of me and so few of you?"

Ray Harryhausen -

"I had to learn to do everything because I couldn't find another kindred soul. Now you see eighty people listed doing the same things I was doing by myself."

Wyatt Earp -

"That nothing's so sacred as honor, and nothing's so loyal as love."

George Armstrong Custer -

"I appeal to you as a soldier to spare me the humiliation of seeing my regiment march to meet the enemy and I not share its dangers."

Gary Cooper -

"I looked at it like this way. To get folks to like you, as a screen player I mean, I figured you had to sort of be their ideal. I don't mean a handsome knight riding a white horse, but a fella who answered the description of a right guy."

Clint Walker -

"There is a lot of stuff now that is in bad taste, and I don't see the necessity for it all. We didn't have to do it in our time, and they don't have to do it now."

Alan Ladd -

"I think any movie star who refuses autographs has a hell of a nerve."

Peter Falk -

"My father's whole life was work. He had a retail store in Ossining, New York, and I mean, he was down there at 6:15 every morning. The store didn't open until 9, but he hadda be down there. That's all he knew."

Claude Rains -

"Often we'd secretly like to do the very things we discipline ourselves against. Isn't that true? Well, here in the movies I can be as mean, as wicked as I want to - and all without hurting anybody."

Raymond Burr -

"I once had a long relationship with a lady, and wherever I went in the world, if I saw something she would look great in, a gown or gloves or a ring, I always knew what color she liked most. I knew her size, what material she appreciated most, and I spent the whole time buying gifts for her. And I loved her very much."

Soupy Sales -

"I've never done a pretentious show; it's always had a live feeling, the kind of thing that comes across when you don't know what's going to happen next. I've never done anything simply because I thought I could get away with it. I've just wanted to do the funniest show."

Bob Hope -

"When we recall the past, we usually find that it is the simplest things - not the great occasions - that in retrospect give off the greatest glow of happiness."

Bette Davis -

"The only reason anyone goes to Broadway is because they can't get work in the movies."

Charlton Heston -

"Shakespeare is the outstanding example of how that can be done. In all of Shakespeare's plays, no matter what tragic events occur, no matter what rises and falls, we return to stability in the end."

William Shatner -

"I was always working. Maybe you weren't aware of the movies I was making, or the television I was doing, or the shows I was creating, or the books I was writing; there have been thirty. But I have always been solidly at work, running as fast as I can."

Roger Moore -
"My father believed in toughness, honesty, politeness and being on time. All very important lessons."

Timothy Dalton -
"I don't think anyone except the few people who have played James Bond can tell you how strange and special it is and how much your life changes."

Lloyd Bridges -
"Sea Hunt was the first time anyone tackled a show that took place underwater. The stories were sort of exciting for kids, like cops and robbers underwater."

Leonardo DiCaprio -
"I don't think I ever expected anything like an Oscar ever, to tell you the truth. That is not my motivation when I do these roles. I really am motivated by being able to work with great people and create a body of work that I can look back and be proud of."

Bela Lugosi -
"I have never met a vampire personally, but I don't know what might happen tomorrow."

Bram Stoker -
"There are such beings as vampires, some of us have evidence that they exist. Even had we not the proof of our own unhappy experience, the teachings and the records of the past give proof enough for sane peoples."

John Cassavetes -

"I won't call my work entertainment. It's exploring. It's asking questions of people, constantly. 'How much do you feel? How much do you know? Are you aware of this? Can you cope with this?' A good movie will ask you questions you don't already know the answers to. Why would I want to make a film about something I already understand?"

Robert Duvall -

"I've always remembered something Sanford Meisner, my acting teacher, told us. When you create a character, it's like making a chair, except instead of making someting out of wood, you make it out of yourself. That's the actor's craft - using yourself to create a character."

William Holden -

"Aging is an inevitable process. I surely wouldn't want to grow younger. The older you become, the more you know; your bank account of knowledge is much richer."

Jack Nicholson -

"I've never been able to say I've been influenced by a list of artists I like because I like thousands and thousands and I've been influenced in some way by all of them."

Jean Harlow -

"When you lie down with dogs, you get up with fleas."

Oliver Reed -

"I'm not a villain, I've never hurt anyone. I'm just a tawdry character who explodes now and again."

Richard Harris -

"Marriage is a custom brought about by women who then proceed to live off men and destroy them, completely enveloping the man in a destructive cocoon or eating him away like a poisonous fungus on a tree."

Charles Laughton -

"They can't censor the gleam in my eye"

Scott Glenn -

"I'm sure one reason I became an actor is my basic unwillingness to live one life."

Marcelo Mastroianni -

"Woman is the sun, an extraordinary creature, one that makes the imagination gallop."

Sophia Loren -

"There is a fountain of youth: it is your mind, your talents, the creativity you bring to your life and the lives of people you love. When you learn to tap this source, you will truly have defeated age."

Christopher Lee -

"I've always acknowledged my debt to Hammer. I've always said I'm very grateful to them. They gave me this great opportunity, made me a well known face all over the world for which I am profoundly grateful."

William Castle -

"An expert is a man who tells you a simple thing in a confused way in such a fashion as to make you think the confusion is your own fault."

George A. Romero -

"I grew up on the old EC comic books before the Comics Code in North American and with all sort of good-natured fun. I never had nightmares I think because all of the old horror stuff that I was exposed to was well meaning in a certain sense."

Alfred Hitchcock -

"There is nothing quite so good as burial at sea. It is simple, tidy, and not very incriminating."

Bill Kurtis -

"Movie stars and singers never fully pass away because their images are replayed on film and recordings, over and over."

Richard D. Zanuck -

"In the studios days, the public's perception of movie stars was much different, because the stars were so much less exposed. This made them seem more special, more unearthly. Today they're no longer perceived as different - they've become human, so to speak."

Ingmar Bergman -

"The doors between the old man today and the child are still open, wide open. I can stroll through my grandmother's house and know exactly where the pictures are, the furniture was, how it looked, the voice, the smells. I can move from my bed at night today to my childhood in less than a second."

Cecil B. Demille -

"Man has made 32 million laws since the Commandments were handed down to Moses on Mount Sinai... but he has never improved on God's law."

Francis Ford Coppola -

"I believe that filmmaking - as, probably, is everything - is a game you should play with all your cards, and all your dice, and whatever else you've got. So, each time I make a movie, I give it everything I have. I think everyone should, and I think everyone should do everything they do that way."

Basil Rathbone -

"As one grows older one becomes more critical of oneself and less of other people."

Federico Fellini -

"When I start a picture, I always have a script, but I change it every day. I put in what occurs to me that day out of my imagination. You start on a voyage; you know where you will end up but not what will occur along the way. You want to be surprised."

Alan Hale -

"Reality is determined not by what scientists or anyone else says or believes but by what the evidence reveals to us"

Adam West -

"I never had to say I'm Batman. I showed up. People knew I was Batman"

Tyrone Power -

"I'm sick of all these knights in shining armor parts, I want to do something worthwhile like plays and films that have something to say."

Peter Sellers -

"Women are more difficult to handle than men. It's their minds."

Groucho Marx -

"Man does not control his own fate. The women in his life do that for him."

Don Knotts -

"Mainly, I thought of Barney as a kid. You can always look into the faces of kids and see what they're thinking, if they're happy or sad. That's what I tried to do with Barney."

Hugh Hefner -

"I was very influenced by the musicals and romantic comedies of the 1930s. I admired Gene Harlow and such, which probably explains why, since the end of my marriage, I've dated nothing but a succession of blondes."

Jeffrey Hunter -

"The idea of making pictures abroad is exciting when you're in Hollywood and have never worked in foreign countries. You think you'll get to see the sights and have all the fun that goes with traveling. Actually, you spend so much time on the job that you don't do much else."

Al Pacino -

"The hardest thing about being famous is that people are always nice to you. You're in a conversation and everybody's agreeing with what you're saying - even if you say something totally crazy. You need people who can tell you what you don't want to hear."

John Cazale -

"I sometimes wonder if the inability to find oneself makes one seek oneself in other people, in characters."

James Stewart -

"Frank called me one day and said, 'I have an idea for a movie, why don't you come over and I'll tell you?' So I went over and we sat down and he said, 'This picture starts in heaven'. That shook me."

Buster Crabbe -

"I was never one to think that because you are in the picture business, because you're an actor, you're a special person. Not at all, and I have little regard for any people who act that way. If you're lucky, you bring a little excitement to the world. If you're really lucky, you lend your fame to worthwhile causes -- as I was recently privileged to do raising money for the 1984 Olympics, or promoting healthy activities. Apart from that, you're just another human being, trying to make a living, doing it the best way you possibly can. That's the way I've always operated, and I will continue to do so, just doing the best I can."

Douglas Fairbanks Jr. -

"Curiously enough, I was one of the first to have some say in Hollywood. By sheer accident, I had four successes in a row in the early 30's and, although I was still in my 20's, I demanded and received approval of cast, story and director. I don't know how I got away with it, but I did!"

Leslie Nielsen -

"I've always been part of comedy. One of the things about our family was that if we were reasonably funny with each other, particularly my two brothers and myself, when my father was upset with something you'd want to make sure in some way you made him laugh. Because when he didn't laugh, you were in trouble!"

John Derek -

"I think love and beauty are what life is all about."

Steve Irwin -

"Yeah, for some reason parrots have to bite me. That's their job. I don't know why that is. They've nearly torn my nose off. I've had some really bad parrot bites."

Nick Adams -

" I dreamed all my life of being a movie star. Movies were my life. You had to have an escape when you were raised in a basement. I saw all the James Cagney, Humphrey Bogart and John Garfield pictures. Odds against the world ... that was my meat."

Victor Mature -

"I'm no actor, and I've got 64 pictures to prove it."

Clayton Moore -

"I often meet adults in their 30s, 40s, or 50s who, as soon as they recognize me, suddenly become six years old again."

Christopher Reeve -

"What makes Superman a hero is not that he has power, but that he has the wisdom and the maturity to use the power wisely. From an acting point of view, that's how I approached the part."

Boris Karloff -

"I am a very lucky man. Here I am in my 80th year, and I am still able to earn my bread and butter at my profession. I am one of that very small family of the human race who happens to thoroughly enjoy his work. If I didn't enjoy it, I wouldn't go on."

Rod Serling -

"There is nothing in the dark that isn't there when the lights are on."

Howard Hughes -

"I don't want to own seventy-five percent of Toolco. I want to own one-hundred percent so I'll not have to report to anyone. I'm leaving for New York tomorrow, and I'm going to London and Paris. When I return, I want you to have bought out my grandparents and my uncle."

Paul Newman -

"If you're playing a poker game and you look around the table and and can't tell who the sucker is, it's you."

Humphrey Bogart -

"The only point in making money is, you can tell some big shot where to go."

Edward G. Robinson -

"I know I'm not much on face value, but when it comes to stage value, I'll deliver for you."

Jack Webb -

"Thank God it's ......Friday!"

Howard Hawks -

"I made 'Rio Bravo' with John Wayne. It worked out pretty well and we both liked it, so a few years later we decided to make it again. Worked out pretty good that time, too."

Confucius -

"To know what you know and what you do not know, that is true knowledge."

Albert Einstein -

"When you are courting a nice girl an hour seems like a second. When you sit on a red-hot cinder a second seems like an hour. That's relativity."

Thomas Aquinas -

"The things that we love tell us what we are"

Ayn Rand -

"The question isn't who is going to let me; it's who is going to stop me."

Ronald Reagan -

"Mad or glad, Mr. Reagan is head over heels in love with Mrs. Reagan and can't even imagine a world without her - He loves her."

James Arness -

"I had the pleasure of knowing Ronald Reagan before he became Governor of California. He was a truly great human being and we usually spent our time together reminiscing about mutual friends."

Will Rogers -

"The worst thing that happens to you may be the best thing for you if you don't let it get the best of you."

Spencer Tracy -

"It is up to us to give ourselves recognition. If we wait for it to come from others, we feel resentful when it doesn't, and when it does, we may well reject it."

Henry Ford -

"Life is a series of experiences, each one of which makes us bigger, even though sometimes it is hard to realize this. For the world was built to develop character, and we must learn that the setbacks and grieves which we endure help us in our marching onward."

Sam Peckinpah -

"The end of a picture is always an end of a life."

John Wayne -

"I've always followed my father's advice: he told me, first to always keep my word and, second, to never insult anybody unintentionally. If I insult you, you can be goddamn sure I intend to. And, third, he told me not to go around looking for trouble."

Steve McQueen -

"When I did 'The Great Escape,' I kept thinking, 'If they were making a movie of my life, that's what they'd call it - the great escape."

Robert Shaw -

"I was never really a character actor- I was always a leading man who was always cast as a character. I wanted to be Jack Nicholson or Jean Gabin"

Roy Schneider -

"The important thing is to do good work, no matter what medium you do it in."

Steve Cochran -

"With this puss of mine, I could play a corpse and be accused of overacting. The big secret in playing a gangster in movies is to really believe that the character you are playing is doing no wrong."

George Raft -

"Part of the $10 million I spent on gambling, part on booze and part on women. The rest I spent foolishly."

Elvis Presley -

"It's not how much you have that makes people look up to you, it's who you are."

Richard Boone -

"And in his third essay Herodius (not Herodotus, a mistaken pronunciation, perhaps) said 'We can contend with the evil that men do in the name of evil, but heaven protect us from what they do in the name of good.'"

Bruce Lee -

"You must be shapeless, formless, like water. When you pour water in a cup, it becomes the cup. When you pour water in a bottle, it becomes the bottle. When you pour water in a teapot, it becomes the teapot. Water can drip and it can crash. Become like water my friend."

Mister Rogers –

"In the external scheme of things, shining moments are as brief as the twinkling of an eye, yet such twinklings are what eternity is made of -- moments when we human beings can say "I love you," "I'm proud of you," "I forgive you," "I'm grateful for you." That's what eternity is made of: invisible imperishable good stuff."

Bob Denver -

"Gilligan's Island is wherever you want it to be in your mind."

Andy Griffith -

"If you think and feel what you're supposed to think and feel, hard enough, it'll come out through your eyes - and the camera will see it."

Don Rickles -

"Everything I've ever done in my whole career, people might not know, I've never written anything down on paper."

Jimi Hendrix -

"Even Castles made of sand, fall into the sea, eventually."

Robert Osborne -

"My love of movies started when I was 7 years old, living in a small town, going to the movies all the time, and finding the people in the movies more interesting than the people in my small town. Also, at that time, it wasn't that easy to find out about movies."

Dolph Lundgren -

"There are a lot of great athletes who stop working out, and they get out of shape like everybody else in their 30s and 40s."

Jack LaLanne -

"We don't know all the answers. If we knew all the answers we'd be bored, wouldn't we? We keep looking, searching, trying to get more knowledge."

Vince Lombardi -

"The measure of who we are is what we do with what we have"

Frank Gifford -

"I had three stages of knowing Wellington Mara. He was my boss for a long time and he was a father figure. And finally, as we got older, he was my friend."

Tom Landry -

"Character is the ability of a person to see a positive end of things. This is the hope that a man of character has."

George Halas –

"San Francisco has always been my favorite booing city. I don't mean the people boo louder or longer, but there is a very special intimacy. When they boo you, you know they mean you. Music, that's what it is to me. One time in Kezar Stadium they gave me a standing boo."

Bill Belichick –

"To live in the past is to die in the present."

George Allen Sr. -

"People of mediocre ability sometimes achieve outstanding success because they don't know when to quit. Most men succeed because they are determined to."

Jim Thorpe –

"I give 'em the hip, then I take it away."

Yogi Berra -

"You've got to be very careful if you don't know where you are going, because you might not get there."

Davy Crockett -

"Remember these words when I am dead. First be sure you're right, then go ahead."

Benjamin Franklin -

"Some people die at 25 but aren't buried until 75."

My Dad -

"Show me who your friends are, I will show you who you will become like."

Ernest Hemingway -

"Every man's life ends the same way. It is only the details of how he lived and how he died that distinguish one man from another."

Franklin D. Roosevelt -

"When you reach the end of your rope, tie a knot in it and hang on."

Winston Churchill –

"You will never reach your destination if you stop and throw stones at every dog that barks."

John Keats -

«I love you the more in that I believe you had liked me for my own sake and for nothing else.»

Henry David Thoreau -

"Live your beliefs and you can turn the world around"

John Muir -

"The power of imagination makes us infinite"

Shakespeare -

"There is a tide in the affairs of men, which taken at the flood, leads on to fortune. Omitted, all the voyage of their life is bound in shallows and in miseries. On such a full sea are we now afloat. And we must take the current when it serves, or lose our ventures."

Walt Disney -

"Mickey Mouse popped out of my mind onto a drawing pad 20 years ago on a train ride from Manhattan to Hollywood at a time when business fortunes of my brother Roy and myself were at lowest ebb and disaster seemed right around the corner."

Peter Pan -

"You know that place between sleep and awake, the place where you can still remember dreaming? That's where I'll always love you. That's where I will always be waiting."

Johnathan Livingston Seagull -

"For each of them, the most important thing in living was to reach out and touch perfection in that which they most love to do, and that was to fly."

Japanese Proverb -

"Fall seven times and stand up eight."

Plato -

"Love is the joy of the good, the wonder of the wise, the amazement of the Gods."

Here are some of the quotes by or attributed to **James Dean**:

"I really don't know who I am..but it really doesn't matter."

"You gotta try your luck at least once a day, because you could be going around lucky all day and not even know it."

"Dream As If You'll Live Forever. Live as if you'll die today."

"The gratification comes in the doing, not in the results."

"Genius would have it that we swim in sand. We are fish and we drown."

"Forgive quickly, kiss slowly, love truly, laugh uncontrollably."

"Being a good actor isn't easy, being a good man is even harder, I want to be both before I'm done. "

"Only the gentle are ever really strong."

"Being an actor is the loneliest thing in the world. You are all alone with your concentration and imagination, and that's all you have."

"I also became close to nature, and am now able to appreciate the beauty with which this world is endowed."

"Trust and belief are two prime considerations. You must not allow yourself to be opinionated."

"To grasp the full significance of life is the actor's duty; to interpret it his problem; and to express it his dedication."

"To me, acting is the most logical way for people's neuroses to manifest themselves, in this great need we all have to express ourselves."

"There is no way to be truly great in this world. We are all impaled on the crook of conditioning."

"And Never Regret Anything That Makes You Smile."

"You are who you are meant to be. Dance as if no one's watching. Love as if it's all you know."

"If a man can bridge the gap between life and death, if he can live on after he's dead, then maybe he was a great man."

Then we have a quote about Jimmy from his true love,

..."He wanted me to love him unconditionally, but Jimmy was not able to love someone else in return ... it was the troubled boy that wanted to be loved very badly. I loved Jimmy as I have loved no one else in my life, but I could not give him the enormous amount that he needed. Loving Jimmy was something that could empty a person".... Pier Angeli

..........and finally the final profound quote;

Vincent Price -

"Right at this moment, I only want silence. I believe that the end of life is silence in the love people have for you. I've actually been running through what people have said about the end. Religion says that the end is one thing, because it serves their purpose. But great thinkers alike haven't always agreed. Shakespeare knew how to say it better than anyone else. Hamlet says 'The rest is silence.' And when you think of the noises of everyday life, you realize how particularly desirable that is. Silence."

CHAPTER 7

Academy Awards— Misery Loves Company

It seems that the Academy of Motion Picture Arts and Sciences has made a practice of not recognizing some of Hollywood's greatest actors, actresses and even producers and directors. Of course everyone most definitely has different and varied tastes when it comes to not only what they feel are great movies but also great performances by their favorite actor or actress. The problem is when a movie or a performance is evaluated by the many critics of the motion picture art form who are paid handsomely to give their critical views of that movie or performance, and the majority agree that it is Academy Award material. Add to that fact that in conjunction with the critics' views the majority of the movie going public also agree that the movie or performance in question is deserving of at the least a nomination.

In the case of Marilyn Monroe there have been far too many of Marilyn's performances that truly fit that category.. The arguments have always been related to her personality and demeanor involving multiple on-set problems. Today what really matters is how Marilyn Monroe's performance stand up against her critics, and what were the other reasons that Marilyn Monroe and countless other movie stars who also were completely overlooked. There have been far too many of these so called snubs by the Academy of Motion Picture Arts and Sciences and many have nothing to do with the quality of the movie or performance. It is unfortunate that even the name of the organization that is representing the motion picture industry contains a contradiction, the word Sciences infers a scientific analysis. However there is much more of a personal view and individual opinions that drive the voting process. Even in the golden years of Hollywood the Oscars were becoming a popularity contest and if you as an actor, actress or producer or director stepped on the wrong toes, it was evident you had no chance of even getting nominated, and a win of the cherished Oscar was completely out of the question. Most if not all of the iconic stars of the golden years of Hollywood are long since gone but the legacy they left behind is in many cases a sad one when you realize how they were never afforded the opportunity to stand before their peers and receive the accolades they deserved. The names read like a list of the greatest stars that ever graced the motion picture screen, and when you peruse though the list I am certain you will be shocked at the names that appear on it. Your first impression will most definitely be, "I always was sure that him or her got an Oscar for...." That's right it is a very sad part of Hollywood that until now is buried in the past but needs to be addressed for the sake of what these individuals gave to the industry that has evolved into a medium that produces inferior products that will never be able to compare to the art form that bears its name. If those actors and actresses were here today I am certain that they would all have stories of how disappointed they were and how difficult it was to keep their feeling locked up inside when the nominations were read year after year and they were overlooked. Everyone who prides themselves and the work that they do wants a so called pat on the back, and in the case of the

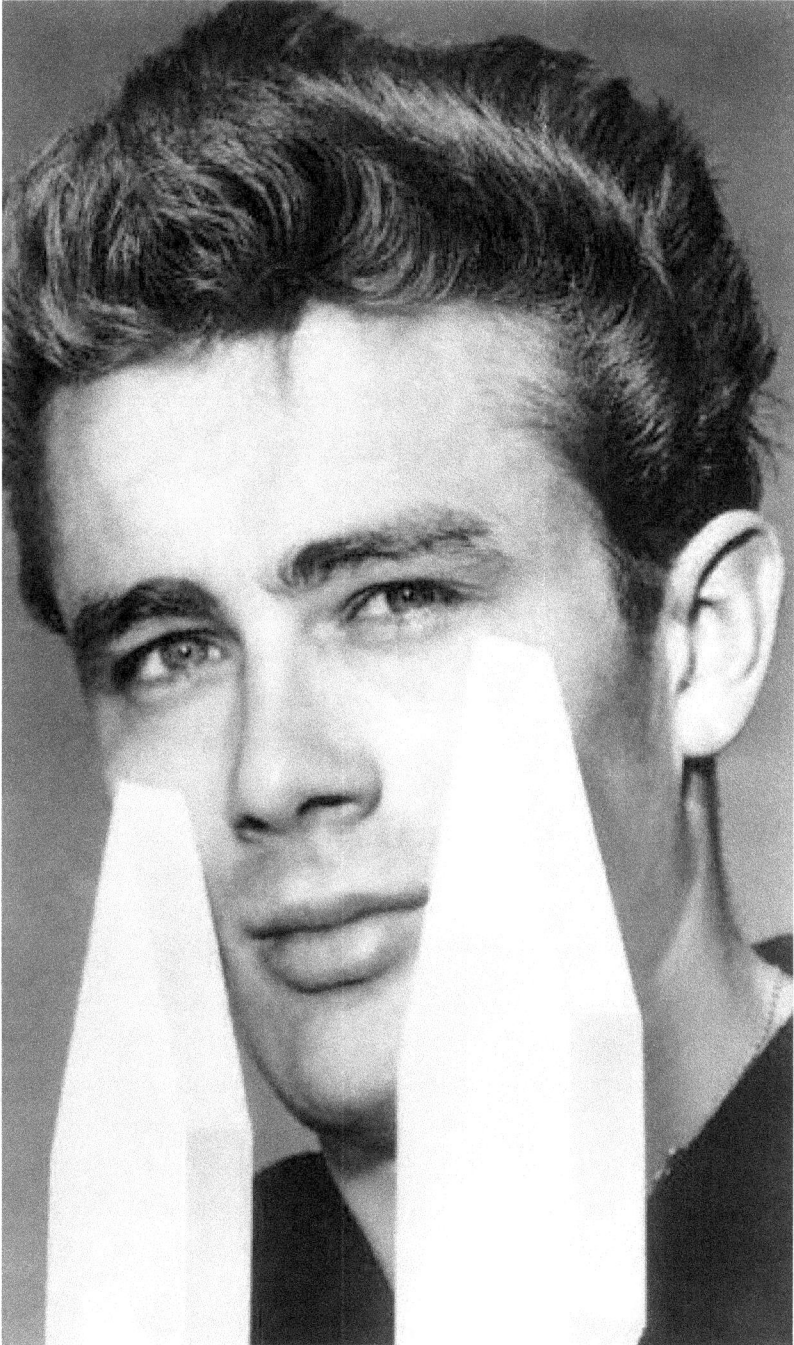

Oscars that "pat" meant not only more starring roles but ones that were sought after by their peers. There was also another factor that most definitely played a part in who was going to get the nomination, that factor had to do with the studio heads. Every studio was led by unique personalities that brought to their corporation a style of management that could virtually make or break a career. The ones that come to mind are Warner Brothers Studios, managed by four head strong brothers, Jack, Harry, Sam and Albert. It was no secret they were not happy with one of their biggest stars, Errol Flynn. Even though Errol Flynn was the biggest money making machine for Warner Brothers Studio for almost a decade, all of the brothers really didn't like his antics off the movie set. Many other studios wanted to borrow, so to speak, Errol for some roles that were tailor made for an actor of his caliber but the Warners' always said absolutely not. Their roles were ones that perhaps would get the actor who portrayed them a nod for an Oscar nomination and that was the very last thing that Jack Warner in particular wanted for Errol. It is ironic that one of Jack Warner's quotes relative to Errol Flynn actually is a testimony of the complete opposite of how Jack Warner treated and spoke of Errol as a person. Jack once said, " When you see a meteor stab the sky, or a bomb explode, or a fire sweep across a dry hillside, the picture is vivid and remains in your mind. So it was with Errol....he was all the heroes in one magnificent, sexy, animal package....he showered an audience with sparks when he laughed, when he fought, or when he loved. I just wish we had someone around today half as good as Flynn." The Warner Brothers were wired in to the Academy and when it came time for the ballots it was almost a certainty that Jack in particular made sure Errol's name was always omitted, even though he lamented in the previous quote of a spectacular motion picture actor. Another major studio was Metro-Goldwyn-Mayer, commonly known as MGM and was once the largest and most glamorous of film studios. MGM was founded in 1924 when the entertainment entrepreneur Marcus Loew acquired three other production companies, Metro Pictures, Louis B Mayer Pictures and Goldwyn Pictures Corporation. The name Loew most certainly will come to mind because it was Marcus Loew who owned Loew's movie

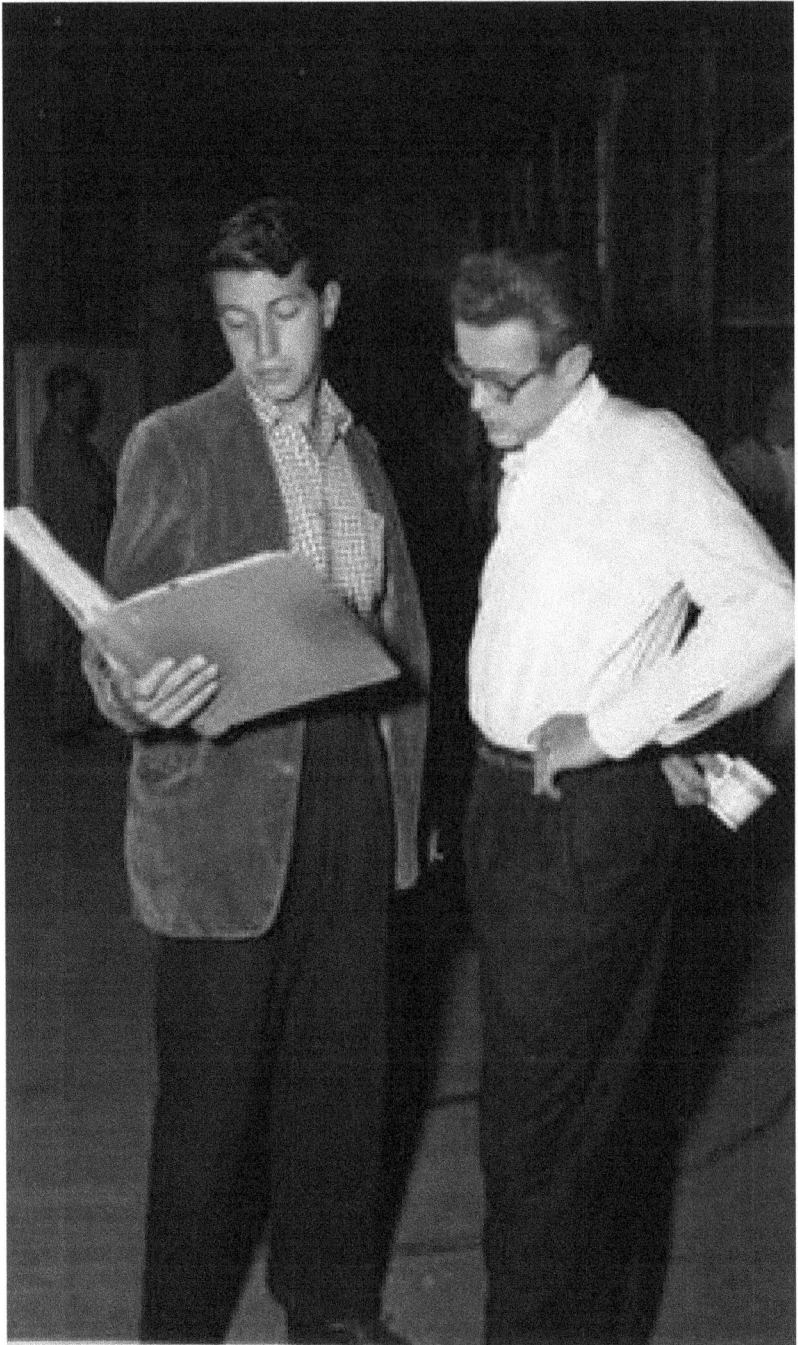

theaters. His studio MGM also had a stable of iconic actors and actresses and unfortunately Mr. Loew never go to see how big his studio, MGM would become because in 1927 only three years after he formed MGM, Marcus died of a heart attack. His studio was getting very big and after his death control of Loew's passed to Nicholas Schenck. It was no secret that may people including Louis B. Mayer referred to him as "Mr. Skunk." He was just one more studio head who was instrumental in who was nominated for Oscars. Another one of the five big original motion picture studios was RKO, Radio-Keith-Orpheum Pictures who not only produced movies but also distributed them. The studio was formed after the Keith-Albee-Orpheum also known as the KAO theater chain and Joseph Kennedy's FBO studio were acquired by RCA in 1928. The then head of RCA, David Sarnoff completed the merger and twenty years later Howard Hughes took over RKO. Some of the many highlights included the release of *King Kong* in 1933, numerous Fred Astaire and Ginger Rogers musicals and of course *Citizen Kane* in 1941. Even though *Citizen Kane* is still regarded as the greatest movie of all time, Orson Welles in the title role was nominated for best actor but lost to Gary Cooper in *Sergeant York*. *Citizen Kane* lost to *How Green was My Valley* in the best picture category. Some of the other studios who were also guilty of playing favorites when it came to the Oscars were Universal Studios and Columbia Pictures. In some unique movie history it can be noted that not one but three of Universal Studios films have the distinction of being the highest grossing film upon its release. The unusual fact relative to all three of the films is not one of them was awarded the best picture Oscar and only two of the three were even nominated. *Jaws* and *E.T. The Extra Terrestrial* were both nominated for best picture but the third film, *Jurassic Park* failed to get the best picture nomination but did in fact score a perfect three out of three in Oscar wins for, Best Visual Effects, Best Sound Mixing and Best Sound Editing. It is quite obvious that Marilyn Monroe was by no means alone when it came to her Oscar snubs. It most certainly has to do with many factors which contribute to both the nomination process as well as the overall final selection process. When you hear the name Marilyn Monroe or see it in print many images immediately enter your mind. the one characteristic that most likely stands out is her voluptuous and extremely beautiful appearance. then perhaps you will remember her in one of her famous movie appearances. Marilyn Monroe was most definitely an asset to any studio that was lucky enough to have her on their roster of movie stars. Most if not all of the movies that Marilyn Monroe appeared in before her most untimely passing were major box office successes. From a critical point of view a few of the performances Marilyn gave did in fact get rave reviews, from some of the most acclaimed reviewers of her day. When it came time for the holy grail of the movie awards, the Oscars, Marilyn was always absent from the ballots. Marilyn Monroe was never even nominated for an Oscar, even though on more than one occasion she turned in a performance that was deserving of at the least a nomination. Marilyn Monroe, Errol Flynn and James Dean joined a group of some of the best actors and actresses who never won an Oscar and the majority of these household names were never even nominated. The names of these Hollywood giants who were overlooked reads like a who's who of movie star royalty. Iconic stars like Judy Garland, Tony Curtis, and Errol Flynn. Then there is all three of greatest horror stars of all time, Bela Lugosi, Boris Karloff and Vincent Price. However there are literally hundreds of others who have either been nominated and lost, and those who have never even been nominated regardless of their iconic status as well as their acting ability. In order to fully grasp how enormous the list is and the familiar names that are on it these are the stars who were never nominated. Of course there is Marilyn Monroe and Errol Flynn but how about Joseph Cotten, Peter Lorre, Mia Farrow, Kim Novak, Maureen O'Hara, Edward G. Robinson, John Barrymore, and Alan Ladd. Of course every actor and actress might not warrant a nomination but the previous list had some really great performances attached to the names. Continuing with the ones who were never nominating, here is Zero Mostel, Douglas Fairbanks, Sr. and his son Douglas Fairbanks, Jr. The greatest comedian of all time, W.C. Fields, and another iconic comedian Bob Hope, not to mention Jerry Lewis and Buster Keaton. Leading men are on the list, Tyrone Power, Ronald Reagan, Will Rogers, Robert Taylor, Robert

Young, Glenn Ford, Martin Sheen, Eli Wallach, and Fred MacMurray. What a list of leading actresses share that dubious distinction, Jean Harlow, Rita Hayworth, Ida Lupino, Shirley Temple, and Tallulah Bankhead. Then there are the actors and actresses who did manage to get nominated but never won. This list has the number of times they were nominated in parenthesis. With the distinction of having the most nominations as an actor, we begin with the actors, Peter O'Toole (8), Richard Burton (7), Arthur Kennedy (5), and Albert Finney (5). Actresses who were passed over but nominated are, Deborah Kerr (6), Glenn Close (6), Thelma Ritter (6), Irene Dunn (5) and Greta Garbo (4). There are many, many more famous celebrities who managed to make you laugh, brought tears to your eyes and most definitely swept you away to distant places in both your hearts and minds, but as far as Hollywood was concerned their performances were not deserving of an Oscar. The list goes on with, some of your favorite stars, Fred Astaire (1), Charles Bickford (3), Maurice Chevalier (2), Montgomery Clift (4), Kirk Douglas (3), Lillian Gish (1), Cary Grant (2), Angela Lansbury (3), Piper Laurie (3), James Mason (3), Agnes Moorehead (4), Gena Rowlands (2), Rosalind Russell (4), Peter Sellers (2), Barbara Stanwyck (4), Orson Welles (1), Richard Widmark (1) and John Cassavetes (1). Some of these famous actors and actresses also were sadly overlooked, Lee J. Cobb (2), Raymond Massey (1), Marcello Mastroianni (3), Steve McQueen (1), Adolphe Menjou (1), Burgess Meredith (2), Robert Mitchum (1), Robert Montgomery (2), Tony Curtis (1), Tom Cruise (3), James Dean (2), Clint Eastwood (1), John Garfield (2), Walter Pidgeon (2), William Powell (3), Claude Rains (4), Basil Rathbone (2), Robert Shaw (1), Max Von Sydow (2), Clifton Webb (3), and James Whitmore (2). There are even more famous actresses and here they are, Jane Alexander (4), Judith Anderson (1), Lauren Bacall (1), Marlene Dietrich (1), Ava Gardner (1), Judy Garland (2), Elsa Lanchester (2), Janet Leigh (1), Marsha Mason (4), Merle Oberon (1), Eleanor Parker (3), Michelle Pfeiffer (3), Debbie Reynolds (1), Gene Simmons (2), Kim Stanley (2), Gloria Swanson (3), Gene Tierney (1), Lana Turner (1), Liv Ullmann (2), Tuesday Weld (1), Natalie Wood (3), and Deborah Winger (3). These great actors and actresses brought to life countless

characters that will be forever etched in every movie goers memory. There will never be another Kane, and there will never be another movie like *Citizen Kane* or *Spartacus*, with a convincing Kurt Douglas in the title role. You will always see Dorothy, a young Judy Garland in the *Wizard of Oz*, following the yellow brick road and proclaiming so vividly, "there's no place like home". How many times have you witnessed Robert Shaw as Quint being devoured by a giant shark in *Jaws*. He played Blondie in *The Good, The Bad and The Ugly* or Marshall Jed Cooper in *Hang em High*, as well as Inspector Harry Callahan, in *Dirty Harry* but Clint Eastwood found out repeatedly, apparently these roles were not good enough. Dracula, an iconic portrayal by Bela Lugosi, Frankenstein, and The Mummy, both strikingly real roles by Boris Karloff. The many characters brought to life by the stoic Vincent Price, such a Professor Henry Jarrod, in *The House of Wax*, Francois Delambre, in *The Fly* and *The Return of the Fly*, Roderick Usher, in *The House of Usher*, Nicholas Medina in *The Pit and the Pendulum*, and Frederick Loren in *The House on Haunted Hill*, still haunt your memory. For sheer drama how about the character Cal Trask, in *East of Eden* or Jim Stark, *The Rebel Without a Cause* or Jett Rink, in *Giant*. These were this actor's only movie characters but each and every one was more than memorable, still no Oscar came his way, he was James Dean. There were the earie gangsters such as Tommy Udo a creepy character Richard Widmark created who sent chills up your spine in *Kiss of Death*, how about the characters Rico in *Little Caesar* and Johnny Rocco, in *Key Largo* brought to life with right on realism, only Edward G. Robinson could bring. This actors career spanned six decades, but everyone remembers him as the fight promotor Mickey Goodmill in *Rocky*, the raspy cantankerous Burgess Meredith failed to snatch Oscar. Even though he was the definitive Sherlock Holmes, the South African born Basil Rathbone almost got the Oscar in two dramas as Tybalt in *Romeo and Juliet* and King Louis XI, in *If I Were King*, almost. This actress was one of Hollywood's brightest and beautiful stars but Ava Gardner couldn't bring home an Oscar as Honey Bear Kelly in *Mogambo*. Three unforgettable roles, first opposite James Dean as Judy, in *Rebel Without a Cause*, then the girl Warren Beatty loved as "Deanie" Loomis, in *Splendor in the Grass*, finally as Angie Rossini Steve McQueen's love interest in *Love with the Proper Stranger* left Natalie Wood without the gold. When you get nominated for an Oscar four times and lose four times you wonder what you have to do to win an Oscar. Such was the case of Claude Rains who played his roles to the hilt, first loss was as Senator Joseph Harrison Paine in the great motion picture, *Mr. Smith Goes to Washington,* he followed that performance with a role in *Casablanca* as Captain Louis Renault. Only two years later Rains was nominated again playing Job Skeffington in *Mr. Skeffinton,* then finally in *Notorious* the Alfred Hitchcock thriller as Alex Sabastian. However two other actors lead the pack in being overlooked when it came to winning an Oscar for their numerous nominated roles, a total of fifteen nominations between them. We start with Peter O'Toole, eight nominations spanning over four decades. His first nomination was for *Lawrence of Arabia* in 1962, and his last was for *Venus* in 2006. In between those two movies Peter was nominated for his roles in, *Becket, The Lion in Winter, Goodbye, Mr. Chips, The Ruling Class, The Stunt Man* and *My Favorite Year.* Then there is Richard Burton who had seven nominations starting off with *My Cousin Rachel,* followed by *The Robe* where he brought to the big screen Marcellus Gallio, then the title character in *Becket.* Two years in a row he was passed over for his performances in *The Spy Who Came in from the Cold,* and *Who's Afraid of Virginia Wolfe.* He turned in a memorable performance as King Henry VIII, in *Anne of a Thousand Days.* His last nomination was for his role as a psychiartrist in *Equus.* Actors are not the only ones who have been nominated several times and passed over, many actresses also share that dubious honor. Marsha Mason for example has been nominated four times, first as Maggie Paul in *Cinderella Liberty,* then as Paula Mcfadden in the *Goodbye Girl.* When she accepted the role of Jennie MacLaine in the hit movie *Chapter Two,* Marsha felt this role would get her an Oscar, it didn't. In the movie, *Only When I Laugh* Marsha played, Georgia, and was nominated a fourth and final time. Another great actress Eleanor Parker was nominated for an Oscar three times. She was extremely versatile and talented, her first nomination was playing the prison inmate, Marie Allen

in *Caged.* The very next year she played Kirk Douglas wife, Mary McLeod in *Detective Story.* Then her portrayal as the opera star Majorie Lawrence in the Oscar winning *Interrupted Melody.* Another great actress who was unable to win an Oscar but was nominated on three occasions was Jane Alexander. In the unforgettable drama *All The Presidents Men,* Jane was nominated for the role as the bookkeeper, Judy Hoback. Two more award winning dramas were able to get Jane noticed and nominated again, *Kramer vs. Kramer* and *Testament.* A pair of extremely gifted actors, one female and the other male each were nominated four times without winning. First, we have Agnes Moorehead who everyone remembers from her T.V. character, Endora in *Bewitched* but she was first nominated for her role in *The Magnificent Ambersons.* She proved it was no fluke when two years later her name was again on the ballot for her role in *Mrs. Parkington.* Once again a few years later in *Johnny Belinda* Agnes was nominated and finally over fifteen years later she wowed the critics in *Hush...Hush, Sweet Charlotte.* Her counterpart of sorts was a special actor by the name of Montgomery Clift. His career was less than twenty years but in his second movie role he managed to get nominated for best actor the movie was *The Search* and Montgomery actually re-wrote the script. He was a unique actor who when playing a role went the distance such is evident when he was nominated for best actor a second time. For his portrayal of George Eastman in *A Place in the Sun,* Montgomery actually spent a night in jail, just one of his many over the top acting techniques. Everyone remembers Montgomery for his role in the great war movie, *From Here to Eternity* but he also was nominated in *Judgement at Nuremberg.* Some actresses were prolific in their quest for the oscar and three were nominated a half of dozen times each. We start with Thelma Ritter who was never really a household name but in a twelve year span was nominated six times, remarkably getting a nomination a record four years in a row. Thelma was nominated in 1950 for her role in *All About Eve,* then in 1951 for wowing audiences in *The Mating Season.* The following year she was again a front runner for the Oscar playing the wise cracking nurse, Clancy in the movie, *With a Song in my Heart.* In 1954 once again Thelma was in top form playing a unique role as Moe, a street peddler in *Pickup on South Street*, most if not all critics agreed she stole the show and was by far going to win an Oscar. She still had something special in the movie *Pillow Talk*, and was nominated once again and finally she played Elizabeth Stroud, the mother of the infamous Robert Stroud, in *The Birdman of Alcatraz*. Six unique and powerful roles, six nominations for the coveted Oscar but like so many great actors and actresses, Thelma Ritter was sadly passed over. Next on the list is Deborah Kerr, a distinguished actress who also was nominated six times and some of the movies she was nominated in are true Hollywood Classics. Movies such as the iconic war film, *From Here to Eternity*, where everyone remembers her beach scene with Burt Lancaster, one of Hollywood's greatest kisses. Deborah held her own as a co-star in *The King and I*, opposite Yul Brynner, as well as playing a nun opposite Robert Mitchum in *Heaven Knows Mr. Allison*, two roles that were easily nominated. The other three nominations Deborah received were first for her role opposite Spencer Tracy as his wife in *Edward, My Son*, most critics agree her finest performance. Then in *Separate Tables* opposite David Niven who won the Oscar in that movie, and finally one more nomination for her role in *The Sundowners*, again opposite Robert Mitchum. The last actress to receive six nominations for the Oscar without winning is Glenn Close. For three straight years Glenn was nominated for her performances in *The World According to Garp*, 1982, then the following year in *The Big Chill* and for her role in the 1984 blockbuster, *The Natural*. Her next three nominations were for completely different roles first as a homicidal maniac in *Fatal Attraction*, then in *Dangerous Liaisons* as as a 17th century seductress, and finally in a unique role as a man in *Albert Nobbs*. Two great male actors also have the distinction of being nominated multiple times, five each to be exact and never brought home the gold. The first is Arthur Kennedy, who received his very first nomination for his role in *Champion* playing Kirk Douglas brother. Then only two years later he was nominated again for his role in *Bright Victory* a 1951 war drama. Later in the decade of the 50's Arthur was nominated three more times, in 1955 for *Trial*, in 1957 for *Peyton Place* and finally in 1958 for *Some Came Running*. Five was an unlucky number for Albert Finney who also failed to win an Oscar even though he also was nominated on five separate occasions. Albert truly brought to life the character of *Tom Jones* in the movie of the same name, then a more different role as Inspector Hercule Poirot in *Murder on the Orient Express*. His versatility came to light again in the movie *The Dresser*, for his third nomination. Over twenty years after *Tom Jones*, Albert was nominated for his unique role in *Under the Volcano*. Then finally but hopefully not Albert Finney's last nomination came fifteen years later in *Erin Brockovich*. Clifton Webb began his acting careen in 1917 but some twenty seven years later he wowed the critics and audiences with his nominated role in *Laura*. He proved his performance was no fluke as he was nominated two times in the next four years for his once again outstanding performances in *The Razor's Edge* and then *Sitting Pretty*. When a movie fan hears the name Ingmar Bergman the first thing that comes to mind is genius. This next actor made eleven films with Mr. Bergman before receiving his first of two nominations for his 1987 role in *Pelle the Conqueror*. Then almost twenty five years later he was nominated more recently in the unique movie *Extremely Loud and Incredibly Close*, his name is Max von Sydow, and in 2013 he has another chance starring in *The Letters*. This next actor had a career in motion pictures that spanned over five decades and starred in some of Hollywood's most iconic films. His name is James Mason and in 1955 he was nominated for his unique role in the hit *A Star is Born*. Over twenty fives years later in 1983 he was nominated for his right on performance in *The Verdict* but failed to win the Oscar. Sandwiched in between those two nominations in 1967 James was nominated for his role in *Georgy Girl*, three great performances that failed to get James Mason an Oscar, that he truly deserved. When the name Inspector Jacques Clouseau is mentioned a smile most likely comes to your face. The Pink Panther movies were some of the funniest productions that were ever made and all hold up today. Peter Sellers brought to life that iconic character but even though he is best remembered for being a comedic genius, Peter was nominated for two Oscars. The first was in the hit *Dr. Strangelove*, and the second was for his role in *Being There*, both failed to win him the gold. Then we have the great Roman

action adventure movie with a cast of Hollywood's biggest male and female stars but one in the title role of *Spartacus* clearly took over the production. Kirk Douglas was never nominated for his role as Spartacus but did manage to get three Academy Award nominations even though he actually should have been nominated a dozen more times. Kirk was nominated in the following movies, *Champion, Bad & The Beautiful* and as a spot on interpretzation of Vincent Van Gogh in *Lust For Life.* Whenever a movie buff thinks of Sophia Loren, the name of her male counterpart, Marcello Mastroianni comes to mind. The pair of Italian actors co-starred in fourteen movies in a span of over twenty years. Marcello had a magical style of acting that was so unassuming and that quality was apparent as he was nominated for an Oscar on three occasions. The first nomination was for his role in *Divorce, Italian Style,* the second for *A Special Day* opposite Sophia Loren and finally for the movie *Dark Eyes.* All three performances were equal in the fact that they all should have brought Marcello an Oscar. In the 1940's and 1950's John Garfield was one of Hollywood's brightest stars. He sadly passed away before the age of forty but managed to get two nominations for an Academy Award. His very first role in 1938 in the movie *Four Daughters* got John a nomination, then several years later he was nominated one last time for his great performance in the movie *Body and Soul.* Errol Flynn, Marilyn Monroe and James Dean, three of Hollywood's greatest stars. As you can see they too were not along when i came to The Quest for an Oscar.

CHAPTER 8

Tributes

When the book, *James Dean: The Quest for an Oscar* was nearing completion, it was important to honor and recognize some forgotten Hollywood stars and personalities. Initially there were only about a half-dozen that warranted inclusion. However, as each star's section was written it was evident that there were many others that should receive a "tribute." Many of the tributes on the pages that follow are virtual unknowns to the modern day movie goers. I suggest that if you read about some that interest you, seek out their body of work. You will not be disappointed. Photos of the stars have been included, remember, "a picture is worth a thousand words."

Tribute to John Holland Cazale

John Holland Cazale was one of the greatest actors that most people are not familiar with. One of the main reasons for that statement being true is, John only appeared in five movies. You might be wondering how relevant can an actor be if he only made five motion pictures. The unusual fact regarding John and his involvement with the movies is quite unique. All five of those motion pictures were nominated for the Academy Award for Best Picture. The five movies were, *The Godfather, The Conversation, The Godfather Part II, Dog Day Afternoon,* and *The Deer Hunter.* John also appeared in archival footage in *The Godfather Part III,* also nominated for Best Picture, making him the only actor to have the distinction. Three of the movies did win the Oscar for Best Motion Picture. They were, *The Godfather, The Godfather Part II* and *The Deer Hunter.* Unfortunately, John passed away at the very young age of only forty two years old. In *The Godfather* movies he played Fredo, it was John's very first starring role in a movie. Perhaps *The Godfather* and *The Godfather Part II* with all of their memorable scenes and characters owe a touch of gratitude to John. His portrayal of Fredo was one that you will never forget. The very memorable first time he appears in the movie is when Al Pacino playing Michael Corleone introduces him to his girlfriend. The scene takes place during the outdoor wedding ceremony for Michael's and Fredo's sister. John Cazale actually steals that moment from Al Pacino and immediately the viewer wants to know more about this interesting character. He was at times throughout the movie, a shy unassuming character. Then a sort of pathetic human being. Two more scenes that stand out are first when he fills in for one of Marlon Brando's bodyguards. Marlon Brando was Don Corleone, Fredo's father. In the scene Brando stops to buy some fruit from a street vendor while Fredo waits in the car. Suddenly two men approach Brando and open fire, hitting him several times. As they flee Fredo fumbles with his gun and then caresses his fallen father. He screams loudly "papa". It is a certainty you will not forget this scene. In another one of Fredo's memorable scenes Michael Corleone travels to Vegas where Fredo is working for Moe Green. They are all together in a sort of meeting when Michael scolds Moe Green for mistreating Fredo. John Cazale seized the moment and even though both Moe Green and Michael are the focal point in the scene Cazale manages to take over and dominate the action in a most memorable way. His look of controversy when he embraces Moe Green while Michael is threatening Green is classical. Even a scene at a nightclub in Havana Cuba is all classic John Cazale as he tries to fool Michael and then realizes he has been discovered as the son of Don Corleone who has betrayed him. In John's final movie *The Deer Hunter,* John gave it everything he had left because soon after he passed away. His eerie performance brought out the best in the rest of the cast and it was his sadness that enveloped the entire production. To be exact John Cazale died even before the completion of the movie *The Deer Hunter.*

In the movie *Dog Day Afternoon* we get a look at John as he portrays the hapless bank robber companion, Sal. You can argue that even though he was not the star. Al Pacino was, John sort of stole the show. Sal, was acting out the part of a big shot but you felt sort of sorry for the pathetic soul who tried to be so much larger. It's all in the stride. He appears to elongate himself with a stride that seems six feet across; and with the flairs, and the machine gun, and the Cuban shoes, it looks even wider. In one classic scene Al Pacino asks Sal what country he'd like to be flown to after the bank robbery they are in the midst of committing. Cazale's answer is "Wyoming." He was dead serious with his answer. He was looking very certain, he was showing a look of vulnerability. Then Al Pacino tells him that Wyoming is not a country, when Sal looks back at him the expressions and mannerisms are truly classical. John Cazale was evolving right before our eyes and he was Sal. Even when Sal asks Al Pacino if he really is going to throw the bodies of the hostages out, Sal said he was ready. He was ready for sure with his mannerisms. A gangster or bank robbery movie never had a character like Sal and it is evident we will never come across the likes of John Cazale ever again.

Tribute to Robert Armstrong

Even if they make another hundred movies about King Kong only one actor associated with the King is unforgettable. The very first time he hit the screen in the original 1933 *King Kong* movie his character Carl Denham was almost bigger than life. Robert Armstrong was another great actor that virtually was flying under the radar. When it came to versatility he was the master and could play any character with realism. However, it will always be the famous last words he uttered in King Kong, "Twas beauty killed the beast", he will be remembered for. Robert also starred in two other great monster movies, *Son of Kong* and *Mighty Joe Young*. His career spanned many decades and he appeared in one hundred and twenty-seven feature films. His television career was also a formidable one with a string of twenty-four episodes in the action adventure State Trooper. He was even a standout in four episodes of the great *Perry Mason* court drama. Robert added cliffhanger serials to his resume and these are some of the best he starred in. *Gang Busters* (1942), *Sky Raiders* (1941), *The Lost Squadron* (1932) and *Adventures of the Flying Cadets* (1943). He was a lovable tough guy who had a distinctive rapid fire delivery and the hard looks to compliment them.

Tribute to Clarence Linden Crabbe ll

Clarence Linden Crabbe was commonly known by his stage name Buster Crabbe. He was an American two-time Olympic swimmer and movie actor. Buster won the 1932 Olympic gold medal for 400-meter freestyle swimming event before breaking into acting. Even though he starred in over one hundred feature films in the 1930s and 1940s and beyond most really don't know much about him. Buster is very unique because he played the title role in the serials *Tarzan the Fearless*, *Flash Gordon* and *Buck Rogers*. Buster Crabbe is the only actor to play Tarzan, Flash Gordon and Buck Rogers. These three heroes were the top three syndicated comic strip heroes of the 1930s. His acting skills and good looks rivaled all the male leads of his era. Buster made countless Western movies and if he was a singing cowboy he would be more well known. There was never an actor who brought a comic book hero to life on the big screen better than Buster. When he landed on the planet Mongo and met the emperor Ming for the first time, you were watching Flash

Gordon coming to life. Quite possibly Buster played Flash a little too good and convincing which led to Hollywood giving him the brush off. Exactly like Errol Flynn, Buster always wore the costumes like he was in the era where the movies took place. Buster became Flash Gordon right before your eyes. He wore a cowboy hat like he was born in it. The most distinctive quality was the way he so effortlessly delivered his lines. Buster's wide range of emotions were also something great actors are born with, he always stole the scene. Unfortunately, like other great actors who were overlooked, it was most likely he played the roles, especially Flash Gordon exactly as the creator of Flash intended, a little too convincing.

Tribute to Darren McGavin

Darren McGavin was an actor who was able to have a great range in all the characters he played regardless of if the roles were in a movie or on television. In 1983 the whole world fell in love with his memorable performance in the

iconic film, *A Christmas Story*. Darren played Mr. Parker the very grumpy but extremely lovable father. Even though at the time he was not very well known, he was paid two million dollars for the role. This made him the highest paid actor of the year. Before that role he starred in about twenty feature films and in 1955 was outstanding in the Frank Sinatra film, *The Man With The Golden Arm*. However, it was always television dramas where Darren made his biggest mark. It's hard to imagine any actor playing multiple characters in a dozen or so television dramas but Darren was in one hundred and twenty eight different TV Shows. There are three that standout and all were highly rated when they aired. The first was Mickey Spillane's, *Mike Hammer*. It ran for two seasons during 1958 and 1959. There were a total of seventy-eight episodes, one better than the next. It can be said that Darren's portrayal of Mike Hammer was the best detective drama on TV of all time. He was able to mix a hard-nosed character with just a touch of humor and suaveness. Darren was next cast in the series *Riverboat* soon after *Mike Hammer* was cancelled in 1959. *Riverboat's* co-star was Burt Reynolds and the forty-four episodes ran from 1959 to 1961. Darren was billed as the ship's captain, Grey Holden. The rumors surrounding the production were that Darren and Burt Reynolds could not get along. Reynolds only lasted a few episodes due to their differences. It would be over a decade later before Darren made another lasting mark on television. Exactly like the success he had with *Mike Hammer*, *Kolchak: The Night Stalker* would become one of the most exciting and influential horror series of all time. The weekly drama was preceded by two made for television movies. The *Night Stalker*, (1972), and *The Night Strangler*, (1973). *Kolchak: The Night Stalker* television series aired weekly in 1974 and 1975. There are however only twenty episodes and they are so popular re-runs can be seen today. The horror stories about supernatural creatures were very well done but it was Darren McGavin's character, Carl Kolchak who kept the audience coming back each week. It can also be noted that the creator of *The X-Files* television series was greatly influenced by *The Night Stalker*. Darren McGavin was the executive producer for Kolchak and his dissatisfaction with the way the show was going led to him to leave the series. If you have never

had the opportunity to watch any of the three aforementioned TV dramas starring Darren, please seek them out. I am convinced you will agree that he was one of the greatest actors who Hollywood really never recognized.

Tribute to Veronica Lake

One of the foremost female stars of the film noir genre was a voluptuous blonde named Veronica Lake. She was the girl with undoubtedly the most beautiful face. She was also famous for her peek-a-boo hairstyle. In the movie *I Married a Witch*, Veronica was able to melt your heart with just a glance. During the 1940's she made a series of memorable film noir movies with Alan Ladd. The two had a dynamic chemistry and Veronica's performances all received critical acclaim.

Veronica Lake also had the distinction of starring in *Sullivan's Travels* (1941). The movie was an instant hit and the reviews she received were far beyond her expectations. Critics of the day raved, "Comedy doesn't come much more classic. If you haven't seen it it's about time you did." Veronica had no name in the movie and was billed as "the girl".

It is difficult to have a favorite movie of hers during that span because they were all highly entertaining. Some of her best movies with Alan Ladd were, *The Glass Key* (1942), *This Gun For Hire* (1942) and *Saigon* (1948). All of the above movies are highly recommended and are a good way to get you introduced to this unique and forgotten star.

Tribute to Kevin McCarthy

The first words that pop in your head if you like old sci-fi movies and the actor Kevin McCarthy is "they're here already." It was near the end of the iconic science fiction classic, *Invasion of the Body Snatchers*. Kevin McCarthy was the star and he uttered those famous words trying to convince motorists on a crowded highway of the existence of aliens. He has 207 roles to his credit in both movie and television dramas. In 1951 he was nominated for the Best Supporting Actor Academy Award for his performance in the movie *Death of a Salesman*. Kevin was a strong proponent of the "Method" school of acting and was a founding member of The Actor's Studio, which was initially formed and taught by Elia Kazan. Some of the more memorable movies he appeared in are, *The Misfits* (1961), *A Gathering of Eagles* (1963), *The Prize* (1963), *Mirage* (1965), and *Hotel* (1967).

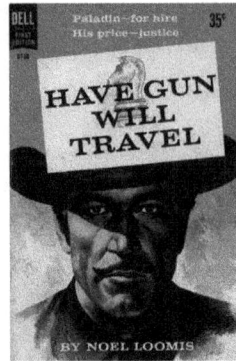

Tribute to Richard Boone

If you were a devote of television Cowboys in the 1950's you most likely were a fan of Richard Boone. He starred in *Have Gun, Will Travel*, as the dark character Paladin. The show was a major hit and Richard received two Emmy nominations. Richard also starred in the hospital television drama, *Medic*. Richard Boone was also a prolific movie actor and starred in three of John Wayne's biggest movies. In the movie *The Alamo*, he played Sam Houston, and with John Wayne starred in, *The Shootist*, and *Big Jake*. Richard appeared in a total of seventy-one movies and also made it back to television in another cowboy drama as *Hec Ramsey*. An unusual twist of fate in his career is that he actually turned down two roles that brought success to other actors. The first was Jack Lord's role in *Hawaii Five-O* and the other was Robert Shaw's role in *The Sting*. His versatility was evident as Marlon Brando asked him to direct the final scenes in the movie *Night of the Following Day*.

Richard was not only a great cowboy villain but he could tackle any role. These are just a few of the movies where he stood out. One of the authors favorite movies he starred in was opposite Paul Newman in *Hombre* (1967). His name Hombre was a memorable bad guy name, perhaps one of the best of all time, Cicero Grimes. Other movies were, *The Raid* (1954), *Man Without a Star* (1954), *The Tall T* (1957), *The War Lord* (1965), *The Arrangement* (1969, Elia Kazan), *The Kremlin Letter* (1970, John Huston) and *The Big Sleep* (1978, Michael Winner).

Tribute to Neville Brand

Most people don't know the name Neville Brand, but with a resume of one hundred thirty-eight movie and television credits, you should be able to recognize his face. Neville Brand jumped off the screen in his very first memorable role in the gangster movie *D.O.A.* (1950). For the remainder of his illustrious career he was cast as a rough and tumble gangster and villain. He was even a bad guy in cowboy movies and had the distinction of being the villain who kills Elvis Presley in *Love Me Tender*. His most famous role came from his portrayal of Al Capone in the television series *The Untouchables*.

Neville reprised his role as Al Capone in the 1961 movie, *The George Raft Story*. He was never without work on the big screen as evidenced by the list of some of his best movies. There was *Tora! Tora! Tora!* (1970), *Birdman of Alcatraz* (1962), *Stalag 17* (1953), *The Ninth Configuration* (1980), *The Tin Star* (1957), *The Desperados* (1969), *The Deadly Trackers* (1973) and *That Darn Cat!* (1965).

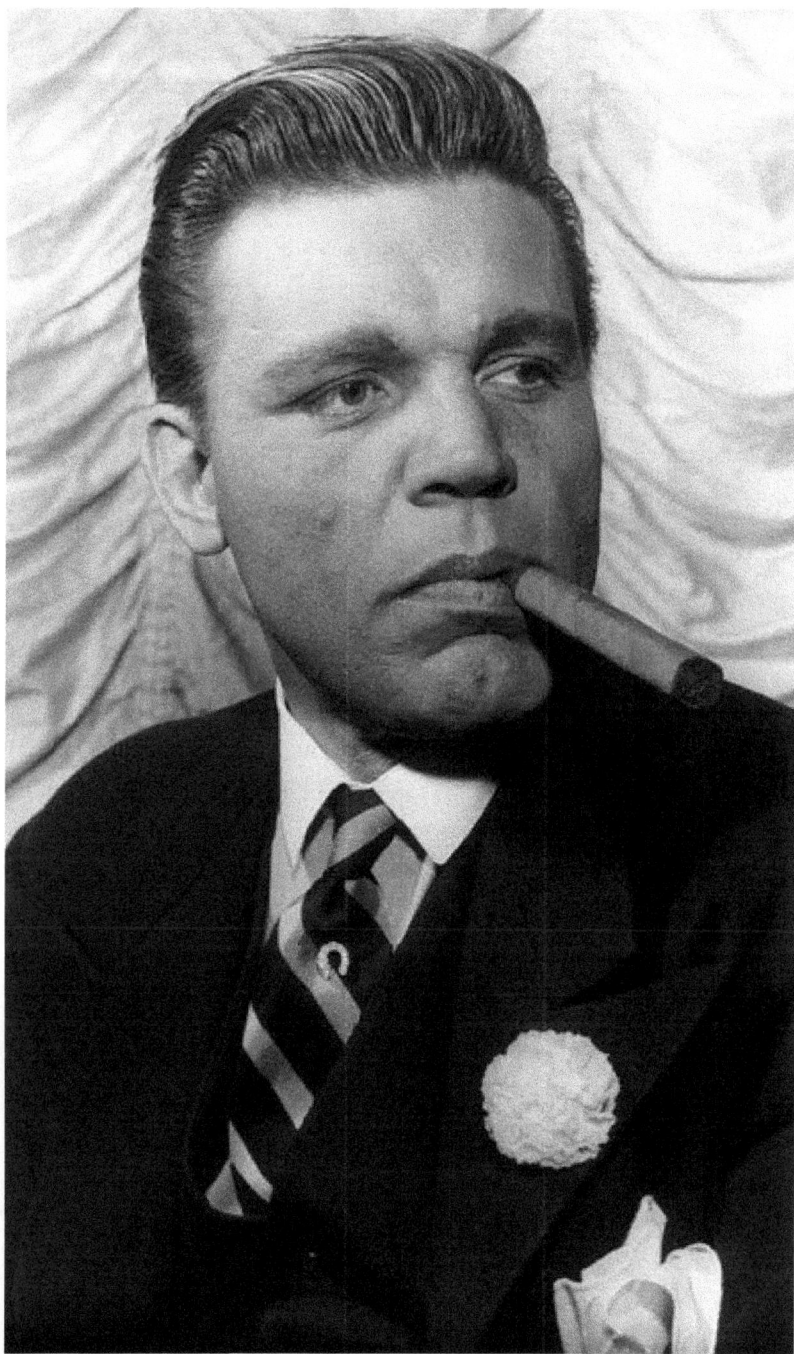

Tribute to Steve Cochran

Steve Cochran was one of the actors that might just remind you of Errol Flynn. Steve had that unique tough guy demeanor, but he could be mean and a pretty boy at the same time. His early career was filled with roles on the stage playing in many Shakespearean productions. He then quickly made his way to Hollywood and had a contract with Warner Brothers Studio. Steve appeared in mostly supporting roles (often playing boxers and gangsters). He appeared in many films, including *The Chase* (1946), *The Best Years of our Lives* (1946), *Copacabana* (1947), *A Song Is Born* (1948), *Highway 301* (1950), *The Damned Don't Cry!* (1950) to name a few. In the great gangster movie, *White Heat* (1949) Steve was James Cagney's henchman, Big Ed Somers, a psychotic character that was his most memorable role. Steve showed his range of characters in the heartbreaking movie *Come Next Spring* (1956). It was the first movie produced by Steve's own production company. He was also no stranger to television starring in *Bonanza*, *The Untouchables*, *Route 66*, *Stoney Burke* and even *The Twilight Zone*.

Tribute to Richard Conte

Richard Conte starred in ninety-five movies and his suaveness and demeanor was ever present. He is perhaps the greatest villain and tough guy ever to grace the film noir genre. Some of the better film noir movies he appeared in confirm that claim. The first of many was, *Cry of the City* (1948) with Victor Mature, *The Sleeping City* (1950), *Under the Gun* (1951), *Hollywood Story* (1951), *The Raging Tide* (1951), *The Blue Gardenia* (1953), *Highway Dragnet* (1954), *The Big Combo* (1955), *New York Confidential* (1955), and *The Brothers Rico* (1957). After his success in film noir he made several movies with Frank Sinatra. The movies were *Oceans 11* (1960), *Tony Rome* (1967) and *Lady in Cement* (1968). In both of the late 1960's movies he was once again a standout as Lieutenant Dave Santini. It seems *The Godfather* is such an iconic film that many actors are remembered for starring in it. Richard Conte was no exception and his portrayal of the crime boss Don Barzini is one of his most memorable performances.

Tribute to George Raft

Most likely the name George Raft may not be too familiar with most of today's movie goers. In the 1930's and 1940's if you wanted to be entertained by watching a gangster movie chances are George Raft was in the cast. He had a rough way of getting his point across and at times was extremely ruthless. George was also a scene stealer and one of the eras best overall male actors. In 1932 he starred in the iconic crime drama *Scarface* opposite Paul Muni. His performance was critically acclaimed and his constant flipping of a coin has become synonymous with him. Some of his other memorable movies are, *Each Dawn I Die* (1939), *They Drive by Night* (1940), T*he House Across* *the Bay* (1940), *Manpower* (1941), *Mr. Ace* (1946) and *Johnny Allegro* (1949). George was even cast as Spats Colombo in the great comedy movie *Some Like It Hot* (1959). When the original *Ocean's 11* (1960) hit the screen there was George holding his own in the star studded cast. It can be noted that George was also a great dancer in some of his other movies, most notably *Bolero* (1934) and *Rumba* (1935). George like so many other great actors turned down some very promising roles. He was offered *High Sierra* (1941) and *The Maltese Falcon* (1941) both were big hits for Humphrey Bogart.

Tribute to Sterling Hayden

He was always playing characters that were larger than life, maybe that's because he was. Sterling Hayden was a tough guy on and off the screen. He had a profound love of the sea exactly like Errol Flynn. Another comparison that can be made between the two men was that both used Hollywood as a means to finance their ships. Sterling traveled in one aptly named *The Wanderer*. The happiest times of his life were spent on the ocean. Even though in *The Godfather* he had a small role as Captain McCluskey, his performance was outstanding and powerful. He starred in seventy-one movies. Some of the more memorable movies he starred in were, *The Asphalt Jungle* which immediately made him a leading man. He was in several other film noir features most notably *The Killing, Crime of Passion* and *Naked Alibi*. Sterling was also comfortable in westerns and some that stand out are, *Johnny Guitar* as Johnny, *The Last Command* as Jim Bowie and *The Iron Sheriff,* as Sam Galt. Another unique role that highlighted his versatility was in *Dr. Strangelove* as General Jack D. Ripper.

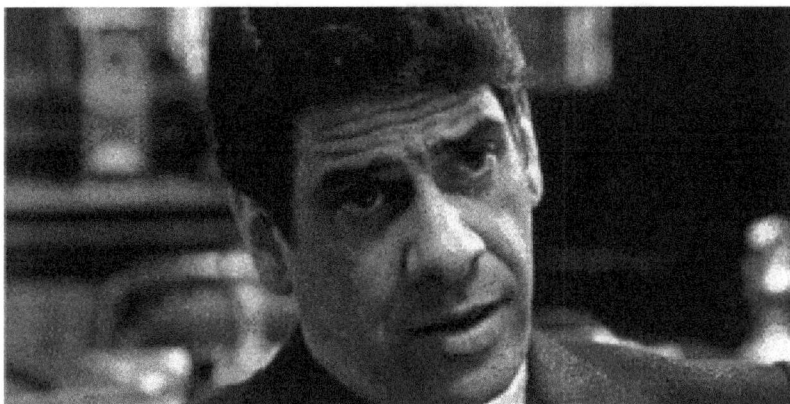

Tribute to Al Lettieri

Al Lettieri only starred in thirty-two movies because he passed away at the very young age of forty-seven. The legacy of being one of the most convincing ruthless and sadistical characters to ever grace the screen belongs to Al. He is best remembered for his almost unbelievable portrayal of Virgil 'The Turk' Sollozzo in *The Godfather*. Prior to that role he menaced the entire cast in the Steve McQueen movie *The Getaway*. Other more memorable movies he starred in were, *Mr. Majestyk* with Charles Bronson, and *McQ* with John Wayne.

Tribute to Steve Reeves and Gordon Scott

These great muscular actors brought to the screen two legendary heroes, *Hercules* by Steve Reeves and *Tarzan* by Gordon Scott. When the very first *Hercules* movie was released in 1958, Steve Reeves spot on depiction of the mythological hero began a whole genre of sword and sandal epics. A few years before that movie in 1955 Gordon Scott brought his version of Tarzan to the screen. The very first Tarzan movie he made was *Tarzan's Hidden Jungle*. In many ways the next five Tarzan films starring Scott cemented his depiction of Tarzan as one of the best. The two even shared the screen in the sword and sandal epic *Duel of the Titans*, as the characters Romulus and Remus. Both actors never made it big in Hollywood but were mainstays in the European movie market. Steve Reeves showed his versatility by playing the lead role in *The Thief of Baghdad* and *Morgan the Pirate*. Steve Reeves is credited in only 23 movies and Gordon Scott is credited in 28 feature films. A special note is the fact that Steve Reeves' sequel to *Hercules*, the movie *Hercules Unchained*, was as good as the original.

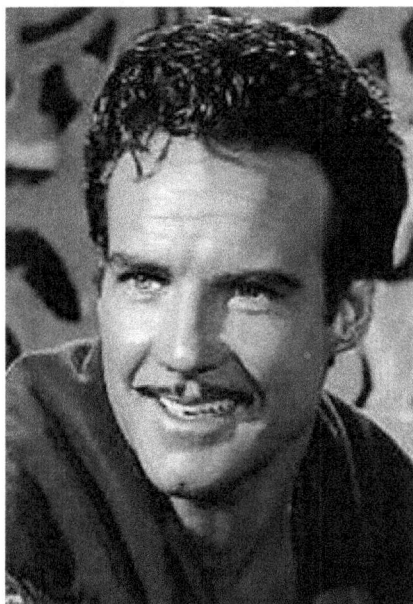

STEVE REEVES

CAPITAINE MORGAN

LYDIA ALFONSI
GIULIO BOSETTI
ANGELO ZANOLLI

UN FILM DE
ANDRE DE TOTH
VALERIE LAGRANGE
IVO GARRANI

ARMAND MESTRAL
CHELO ALONSO

EASTMANCOLOR
CINEMASCOPE

Tribute to Murray Hamilton

The word prolific describes how Murray Hamilton approached all of his 156 movie and television roles. One of those roles was as the mayor in *Jaws*. When faced with the prospect of closing the beaches he said "I don't think you appreciate the gut reaction people have to these things...Martin, It's all psychological. You yell 'Barracuda,' everybody says 'Huh? What?' You yell 'Shark,' we've got a panic on our hands on the Fourth of July." He also played the mayor in the sequel, *Jaws 2*. The two *Jaws* movies were not the only blockbuster movies Murray starred in. There was *Anatomy of a Murder, The Hustler, The Graduate* and *The Amityville Horror*. On television he was in *Rich Man, Poor Man, Perry Mason* and *The Untouchables* to name a few.

Tribute to Robert Shaw

Who can ever forget the first time you saw Quint in the movie Jaws. He was the actor who captured your attention by merely being cantankerous. Many years prior to Jaws, he was in a pirate television show, *The Buccaneers*. Robert played Captain Dan Tempest, and he was the perfect pirate. Ironically the series which aired in 1956 for thirty-nine episodes with Robert Shaw as the pirate captain would be a springboard for his pirate nature. Twenty years later he starred in the big pirate movie *Swashbuckler*. The movie got rave reviews and Hollywood's most famous movie critic, Roger Ebert gave the movie a big thumbs up. Mr. Ebert wrote the following in regard to Robert Shaw's performance. "Robert Shaw demonstrates in *Swashbuckler*, as he did in *Jaws* that apart from his larger skills and ambitions he knows how to be an absolutely first-rate B actor. He's forcible, he's charming, he's physical in a role that calls for few subtleties. And he doesn't ham things up, as so many good actors have been tempted to do in pirate movies. He seems absolutely sincere, and that helps set the film's tone". Those are pretty impressive words of praise coming from a top movie critic. Speaking of the movie *Jaws*, it can be said that one of the greatest movies of all time was made even greater because of

the presence of the character Quint. It was Robert's dynamic interpretation of the character Quint, the grumpy old sea captain that most remember. Robert was the perfect addition to the other main characters, Police Chief Brody played by Roy Schneider and Hooper the marine biologist played by Richard Dreyfus. All three actors were spectacular but the character Quint is the one who was so good and the only one who died at the end. Robert Shaw starred in many other great movies. All of which were special for many reasons but mainly because of the characters he brought to life. He even received an Academy Award nomination for Best Supporting Actor in the movie *A Man for All Seasons*. Some of the other movies he starred in were, *The Sting*, *From Russia With Love*, *Black Sunday*, *The Deep* and *Robin and Marion*.

Tribute to Douglas Fairbanks Jr.

One of Hollywood's greatest action, adventure movies, *Gunga Din* (1939) had three iconic actors in its cast. There was Victor Mclaglen, Cary Grant and Douglas Fairbanks Jr. who virtually stole the show. Douglas Fairbanks Jr. was a charismatic swashbuckling actor who might have been one of Hollywood's greatest leading men if not for a contract dispute with Warner Brothers Studio. He even has a connection to Warner Brothers other great swashbuckler, Errol Flynn. It was Douglas who told Jack Warner about Errol Flynn's potential and to consider him in some upcoming projects. Douglas starred in some memorable action films such as, *The Prisoner of Zenda* (1937), *Rulers of The Sea* (1939), *The Corsican Brothers* (1941), *Sinbad the Sailor* (1947) and *The Fighting O'Flynn* (1949). Douglas was also a war hero and he received the following medals, U.S. Navy's Legion of Merit with V for Valor, the Italian War Cross for Military Valor, The French Legion d'honneur and the Croix de guerre with Palm, the British Distinguished Service Cross and the Silver Star. If that wasn't enough The is also credited as being "Father of the U.S. Navy Beach Jumpers."

Tribute to Gilbert Roland

Gilbert Roland was a charismatic actor who could assimilate into any role and deliver a performance that made both the viewers and critics take notice. His career in movies began as far back as 1923. Most of the characters he portrayed were those of the supporting role category. As you can see by the photos he had very distinctive good looks. That trait was used in the 1933 film *Our Bettors*, where he brought to life in a convincing fashion, Pepe the gigilo. In 1940 he was perfect in the role of Captain Lopez in *The Sea Hawk* opposite Errol Flynn. Some of his other memorable roles were in *We Were Strangers* (1949), *The Bad and the Beautiful* (1952), where Gilbert received a Golden Globe nomination. He received a second Golden Globe nomination in *Cheyenne Autumn* (1964) as the character Dull Knife. There was a movie about of all things sponge divers, *Beneath the 12-Mile Reef* (1953) that Gilbert rolled up his sleeves and played Mike Petrakis. The year was 1952 and Gilbert was cast as Hugo da Silva in the true story *The Miracle of Our Lady of Fatima*. If you have never had the opportunity to view this movie you will be moved by Gilbert's performance as well as the performances of the other actors as well as the theme. He also starred in many television shows but one will always standout, Gilbert as The Cisco Kid.

Tribute to Alan Hale Sr.

One of the most versatile actors of his day Alan Hale Sr. could master any role. He was a very close friend of Errol Flynn and was in many of Errol's greatest movies. Those movies included, *The Prince and the Pauper* (1937), *The Adventures of Robin Hood* (1938), *The Sisters* (1938), *Dodge City* (1939), *The Private Lives of Elizabeth and Essex* (1939), *Virginia City* (1940), *The Sea Hawk* (1940), *Santa Fe Trail* (1940), *Footsteps in the Dark* (1941), *Desperate Journey* (1942), *Gentleman Jim* (1942), *Thank Your Lucky Stars* (1943) and *The Adventures of Don Juan* (1948). There is an interesting bit of trivia regarding Alan. In 1922 he played the character "Little John" in the movie *Robin Hood*. He reprised the role 16 years later in *The Adventures of Robin Hood*. Finally in 1950 he once again played "Little John" in *Rogues of Sherwood Forest*. That is a span of 28 years playing the same character in three different theatrical movies. His son Alan Hale Jr. played "Skipper" on the television hit *Gilligan's Island*. In another bit of Hollywood trivia both father and son played the same character in the movies some 40 years apart. The character was Porthos the musketeer. Alan Hale Sr. played him in the movie *Man in the Iron Mask* (1939) and Alan Hale Jr. played him in the movie *The Fifth Musketeer* (1979). Alan Hale was in a total of 235 movies.

Tribute to Cesar Romero

Cesar Romero can only be described as the ultimate, Latin lover. He was one of Hollywood's special versatile actors both in the movies and on television. Cesar is credited with 202 appearances in both movies and television. His most dynamic performances in the movies ran the gamut of roles. It all began with *The Shadow Laughs* (1933) as Tony Rico. He made 6 *Cisco Kid* feature films and they were all big hits. The first was *The Cisco Kid and the Lady* (1939) followed by *Viva Cisco Kid, Lucky Cisco Kid* and *The Gay Caballero* (all 1940). Then *Romance of the Rio Grande* and finally *Ride on Vaquero* (both 1941). Cesar was able to play tough and sinister gangsters as well. He could dance and play comedy opposite Carmen Miranda in *Week-End in Havana* (1941) and *Springtime in the Rockies* (1942). When it came to playing historical figures in costume dramas Cesar was highly sought after. Darryl Zanuck personally selected Cesar to play opposite Tyrone Power in the historical epic *Captain from Castile* (1947). Then Cesar made his mark on television by playing one of the greatest villains of all time. The show was *Batman* and Cesar played The Joker from 1966-1968 in 22 episodes and one *Batman* feature film. Later in his career he was a regular on the hit television series *Falcon Crest* playing Peter Stavros. He was a main character, Billionaire Greek industrialist in 51 episodes from 1985-1987. Cesar even played a small time criminal in several Walt Disney productions as a nemesis to Kurt Russell.

Tribute to Lee Van Cleef

Lee Van Cleef is perhaps the most recognized villain in both cowboy and gangster movies. His very first movie role was as the silent gunslinger in *High Noon*. That performance highlighted by his unique on screen persona paved the way for countless other parts as a bad guy. Film noir movies that he starred in were all big hits. *Kansas City Confidential* (1952), *Vice Squad* (1953) and *The Big Combo* (1955). Lee appeared in many television shows during the 1950's and 1960's. It was during that time in his career that in 1965 Sergio Leone cast Lee in *For a Few Dollars More*. His co-star was Clint Eastwood and the movie was an instant hit. In 1966 both Lee and Clint starred together in the iconic western *The Good, the Bad and the Ugly*. Lee then became a major star in Spaghetti Westerns most notably the title role in *Sabata* (1969), and *Return of Sabata* (1971). In his career Lee was in 90 movies and 109 television appearances. It can also be noted he died in many of those films.

Tribute to Jack Elam

Here we have an actor that might just defy description. However, the following is only a partial list of the names of the characters he played in the movies. They are, henchman Raymond, Mescal Jack, Gimp, Shotgun, Horseface, Cheesecake, Snaky, Bad Jack Cutter, Crazy Charlie, Rattlesnake, Buckshot and Black Jack Ketchum. With a list of names like these it is evident that Jack was one scary guy. His tough looks were highlighted by a sleepy left eye, coupled with a slow drawl of a voice. Jack was in hundreds of movies and television shows almost always playing a villain. Some of his more memorable roles were in *The Sundowners* (1950), *Kansas City Confidential* (1952), *Vera Cruz* (1954), *Gunfight at the O.K. Corral* (1957), *The Comancheros* (1961) with John Wayne, *4 For Texas* (1963), *The Way West* (1967), *Once Upon a Time in the West* (1968), *Rio Lobo* (1970) with John Wayne and *The Cannonball Run* (1981). Jack also was in many television dramas such as *The Lone Ranger, Gunsmoke, The Rifleman, The Rebel, Have Gun Will Travel, Lawman, Bonanza,* and *The Twilight Zone.*

In 1994, Elam was inducted into the Hall of Great Western Performers of the National Cowboy and Western Heritage Museum.

Tribute to Charles Napier

Charles Napier was one of Hollywood's greatest square jawed tough guys. His career as an actor began after he spent time as a quasi bodyguard for a girl who was auditioning for a Russ Meyer movie. Russ liked his look and raspy voice immediately and Charlie was cast in the Russ Meyer movie, *Cherry, Harry, and Raquel!* (1970). He starred in two other Russ Meyer movies *Supervixens* (1975) and *Beyond the Valley of the Dolls* (1970). Some of the other movies he starred in were *Rambo: First Blood Part ll* (1985), *The Silence of the Lambs* (1991), *The Blues Brothers* (1980), *Married to the Mob,* (1988), and two *Austin Powers* Movies. When it came to television Charlie was in some of the most popular shows. Big name dramas such as *The A-Team, The Rockford Files, B.J. and the Bear, Star Trek* and *Knight Rider*. Charlie even managed to get a small part in the hit HBO show *Curb Your Enthusiasm*. It was a classic scene as Charlie played a barber who assaults and drives Larry David from his barbershop. Charlie's voice was so dynamic he was used as the growls for the *Hulk* T.V. Series. He was cast in 203 movies and television productions which is a major accomplishment. Chances are you knew his face but now you know a little more about the man.

Tribute to Victor Mature

There was an era in Hollywood when biblical movies were very popular. Victor Mature was the one actor that is often associated with that movie genre. He began his career in the movie *The Housekeeper's Daughter* (1939) with a small part. One year later he got the lead in Hal Roach's cave man drama, *One Million B.C.* For the next decade he made sixteen movies, including two great film noir features. The film noir movies were *Kiss of Death* (1947) and *Cry of the City* (1948). Then in 1949 he was the lead in the biblical drama *Samson and Delilah*. Victor is best remembered for his portrayal of the gladiator Demetrius in *The Robe* (1953) and the sequel, *Demetrius and the Gladiators* (1954). Victor retired at the age of only 46 but Neil Simon convinced him to parody himself in the comedy *After the Fox* (1966). He was another actor that Hollywood never really recognized and the 72 movies he made were all highly entertaining and made millions for the studios he worked for.

Tribute to Groucho Marx

There are too many things to talk about that the distinctive Groucho Marx achieved as a consummate entertainer. Everyone knows about the famous comedy team The Marx Brothers but it was Groucho who always stood out. When Groucho had his television show *You Bet Your Life* the introduction said it all. "The One...The Only...Groucho Marx." If you liked Groucho he was so special that just seeing him with his cigar was enough to make you laugh. He had impeccable wit and timing and none of it was ever rehearsed. Groucho made thirteen motion pictures with his brothers and many more as a solo artist. The most famous and classic Marx Brothers movies were, *Animal Crackers* (1930), *Duck Soup* (1933), *A Night at the Opera* (1935), *A Day at the Races* (1937), *Room Service* (1938), *A Night in Casablanca* (1946) and *Love Happy* (1949). Groucho even has the very unique distinction of having The Groucho Marx Papers, listed in The Library of Congress. When Groucho was in the hospital and extremely frail and ill the following occurred. A nurse was about to take his temperature with a thermometer. She explained that she wanted to see if he had a temperature, Groucho said, "Don't be silly—

everybody has a temperature." Groucho Marx was a comedian, writer, actor in the movies, on the stage and television and the radio. He is considered to be the greatest comedian of the modern era. One of his quotes says it all, " I have had a perfectly wonderful evening, but this wasn't it."

Tribute to Phil Silvers

There was only one Sgt. Ernie Bilko and there could be only one actor who could bring him to life. Phil Silvers was perhaps the most unique comic genius of all time. The interesting thing regarding Phil Silvers comedic expertise is that he never did stand up comedy. The show where Phil played Sgt.Bilko was *The Phil Silvers Show*. The *Radio Times Guide to TV Comedy* voted it the number one Sitcom of all time. Phil was not only a major star on television but he was in many motion pictures and an award winning stage performer. He has the distinction of being the first leading actor to win a Tony Award in a revival of a musical. The play was *A Funny Thing Happened on the Way to the Forum* (1972). In 1952 he won his first Tony Award for his outstanding performance in *Top Banana*. Some of the movies he appeared in were, *All Through the Night* (1942) with Humphrey Bogart, *Four Jill's in a Jeep* (1944), *Top Banana* (1954), *It's a Mad, Mad, Mad, Mad World* (1963), *A Funny Thing Happened on the Way to the Forum* (1966), *A Guide for the Married Man* (1967) and *The Chicken Chronicles* (1977). Phil's legacy includes the little known fact that the Hanna-Barbera cartoon *Top Cat* is based on The Phil Silvers Show. Phil was also featured in Marilyn Monroe's last film the unfinished *Something's Got to Give* (1962). Phil was a guest in the popular British, *Carry On* movies and his salary was the largest ever £30,000 of any actor in the series, and that was 1967.

Tribute to Elvis Presley

Elvis Presley was the greatest singer and showman of all time. There was however another side to Elvis and it happened to be his ultimate passion. Elvis starred in 31 feature films. Most critics were hard on Elvis from the very first movie he made, *Love Me Tender* (1956) to his last movie, *Change of Habit* (1969). In between those two films there are some outstanding performances that slipped through the cracks. However, Elvis debut in *Love Me Tender* was a big surprise by the way he handled the role. If there is one criticism regarding that debut performance, it was Elvis was trying a little too hard. There are several movies that stand out and Elvis performance in them was very close to getting him recognized as an actor. Being Elvis most likely was one of the main reasons why he was always overlooked and in some cases ridiculed. *King Creole* (1958) is one of the Elvis movies where Elvis proved he could play a convincing dramatic role. There were also standout performances in *Jailhouse Rock* (1957), *Blue Hawaii* (1961), and of course *Viva Las Vegas* (1954). Elvis even made a pretty good cowboy as he proved in *Flaming Star* (1960). One of the roadblocks in Elvis's movie career had a tragic ending.

The movie that might have cemented Elvis as a serious actor was, *A Star is Born* (1976). The star of the movie Barbara Streisand actually went to Las Vegas to convince Elvis he should accept the male lead in the film. Elvis desperately wanted to take the offer but circumstances and the intervention of his manager squashed the deal. Would the role in *A Star is Born* proved to be Elvis breakthrough performance in the movies? Unfortunately it is a burning question that will never be answered.

Tribute to Massimo Troisi

Massimo Troisi was an Italian actor, film director and most of all a poet.
If you are not familiar with his name watch the movie *Il Postino*. In a strange
twist of fate Massimo died just twelve hours after the final scene in the movie
was completed, he was only 41 years of age.

Many people think that the movie ends with the death of the main
character because Massimo had died. It was not true. That's how we wrote
it. And when Mario Cecchi Gori, the producer, asked if ending with a death
was not too depressing, Massimo said: "No, Mario. Because there is no death
in the movies."

And he was right.

Throughout the movie *Il Postino* we are constantly reminded to be
sensitive to our surroundings and love, to follow our hearts desires and be
alive. Love is the greatest of all gifts and Massimo is alive in our hearts. Il
Postino is the most romantic and melancholic movie ever made, true love is
everlasting.

CHAPTER 9

James Dean
Trading Card Collection

THE COMPLETE NARRATIVE on the reverse of the fifty card set.

Even though Cal Trask, Jim Stark, and Jett Rink were the only three leading characters James Dean ever portrayed on the big screen, each personality he created stands alone as a definitive work of art. The story of James Dean's life can best be told by drawing from these roles and relating them to incidences surrounding his powerful influence on everyone that he came into contact with, both on and off the screen. James Byron Dean was born February 8, 1931 at 2 AM in the Seven Gables Apartments, 320 E. 4th St., Marion, Indiana. The story begins.

In 1935 the Dean family moved from Indiana to California, and what had been a rather happy childhood for Jimmy was marred by the untimely death of his mother in 1940. Jimmy then moved back to Fairmont, Indiana to live with his aunt and uncle. His character took shape in school as he was an all-around good student and excelled in athletics as well as the dramatic rolls he portrays so effortlessly. While in high school he played on both the basketball and baseball teams and even held a pole vault record as a member of the track team. In 1947, as a sophomore in Fairmount High School, Jimmy had rolls in three different school productions. It was obvious to those who saw his early work that Jimmy was special, a natural in every sense of the word.

In April 14, 1949, Jimmy made the headlines of the local Fairmount News: "F.H.S. student wins state meets". His photograph was underneath the headline and the column read, "James Dean first place winner in dramatic speaking". This achievement was indicative of Jimmy's energy, because he always had to be the best at everything and was never one to sit still. He would try almost anything and once nearly broke his back with a homemade elevator he had placed at the top of the barn. In another instance he lost his four front teeth after imitating a trapeze artist on a rope.

The first photograph of Jimmy on a motorcycle was at age 17 when his aunt and uncle bought him a small motorized bike called a Czech Whizzer. During that year Jimmy's life revolved mainly around school, his bike, and his obsession with speed. Those who knew him during this period of his life remember him as being very strange and intense. He was very unpredictable and it was the loss of his mother which continued to influence his innermost feelings. The childlike quality of his performances were perhaps his way of immersing himself in his roles.

The day all high school seniors long for, graduation day, in Jimmy's case, it was May 16, 1949. In one short month, on June 15, 1949, James Dean

left by bus to California where he was met at the bus station by his father in downtown Los Angeles. He enrolled in Santa Monica City College and began his freshman year as a physical education major in January 1950. The college shared grounds with Santa Monica High School, which ironically would be used five years later as the location for Dawson High in "Rebel Without a Cause".

Very little about Jimmy's social life during his college days is well documented. However, he played basketball as a substitute guard and often did announcements on the college FM radio station. The chairwoman of the college's drama department, Jean Owen, immediately recognized Jimmy's talent. She would become a sort of mother figure to Jimmy, the first of many in his life. It was common place for Jimmy to discuss his problems with Jean for hours and it was her who awakened his fascination with Hamlet. She later

said that Jimmy interpreted this role with not only intensity, but extraordinary perceptiveness.

Towards the end of 1950, Jimmy landed his first professional acting job. Jimmy, along with a group of teenagers, danced around the jukebox in the Pepsi-Cola commercial singing "Pepsi-Cola hits the spot...". For this you received $30. But Jimmy soon became restless and in January 1951 withdrew from college. He immediately began attending the drama workshop organized by James Whitmore, an avid exponent of the somewhat notorious "Method" school. This method form of acting required the actor to draw on personal, emotional experiences in developing a character, which was tailor-made for Jimmy.

In 1951 Jimmy got a role in a live TV drama, "Hill Number One". In this original teleplay a group of soldiers during World War II underwent a metamorphosis in which they became Christ's disciples who after the master's crucifixion debated whether they should disband. Jimmy was cast as John the Apostle, the youngest disciple, along with Raymond Burr as Peter and Lief Erickson as Pontius Pilate. During the shooting Jimmy had a bad cold which made his voice unnaturally deep and subsequently more effective for the role. It was during this time a group of Los Angeles schoolgirls formed the first of many James Dean fan clubs named *The Immaculate High James Dean Appreciation Society.*

In the early 1950s acting parts were hard to come by and Jimmy held numerous jobs while awaiting his big break. He worked as an usher at CBS and like most Hollywood hopefuls also worked as a parking lot attendant. Several bit parts came his way doing the summer of 1951 and one particular scene from that time still stands out after all these years. The picture, "Has Anybody Seen My Gal", starring Rock Hudson, has Charles Coburn standing behind the counter in a candy store when Jimmy sits down and says, "Hey,

Gramps I'll have a choc malt, heavy on the choc, plenty of milk, four spoons of malt, two scoops of vanilla ice cream, one mixed, one floating...".

By September of 1951, Jimmy, on the advice of James Whitmore, left Hollywood for New York to look for work in the theater. He arrived in New York with little more than $100 in his pocket, and moved to the YMCA on W. 63rd St. and washed dishes in a bar on W. 45th St. Jimmy was looking for an agent and soon found Jane Deacy at the Louis Schurr Agency. Jane not only became Jimmy's agent until his death, but also became another of the mother figures in Jimmy's life.

In November of 1951 while waiting for new roles, Jimmy got a job as a stunt tester on the game show "Beat The Clock". New York City furnished budding actors with an abundance of perspective opportunities seeing that as many as 30 live drama and comedy show were produced there each week. Jimmy went to virtually all of the open casting calls and at one CBS audition at the Martin Beck Theatre, he met Martin Landau, an actor who was to become one of his closest friends in the city. They soon began to meet at Cromwell's Drugstore, an actor's coffee shop inside the 5th Avenue entrance of the RCA building.

Jimmy did a lot of stage work during 1952, and shortly after his 21st birthday finally got a bit part in the TV drama, "The Web", playing a bellhop. Even though it was just a bit part, Jimmy managed to antagonize producer Frank Heller to the point where only the intervention of the director, significantly a woman, Lela Swift, saved him from being fired. Jimmy's defiant, moody, perfectionist attitude was taking form. It was no secret that he admired Marlon Brando as a rebel and Montgomery Clift as a brooding secretive actor, both being the product of the method school. Ironically, Jimmy emulated the two which formed his own unique persona.

Jimmy was known for doing crazy and unpredictable things throughout

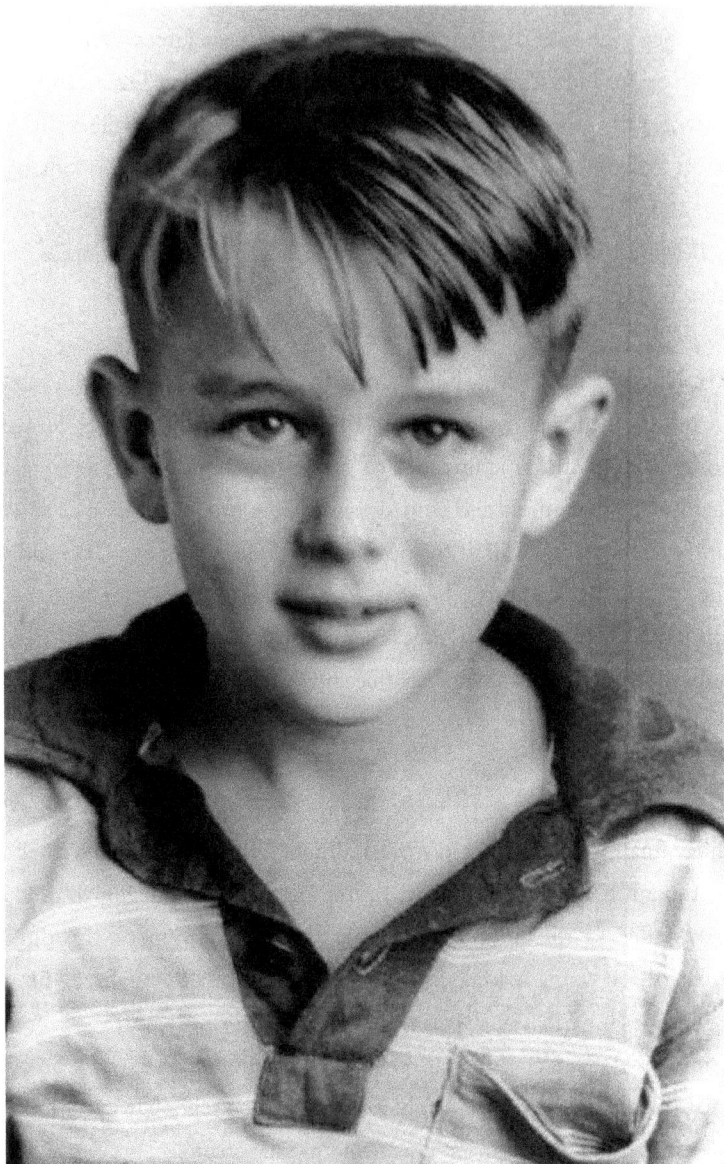

his entire life. One example of his spur of the moment lifestyle occurred while he lived in New York City. Late one October night in 1952, while waiting to hear if he had gotten an audition for the Broadway play, "See The Jaguar", he and his first New York girlfriend, Elizabeth "Dizzy" Sheridan and friend Bill Bast, decided to hitchhike to Fairmount to spend Thanksgiving at the Winslow farm. Dizzy was a dancer he met at the Rehearsal Club, a rooming house for young actresses and dancers. They managed to make the trip in a day and a half.

On December 3, 1952, the play "See the Jaguar" opened at the New York Cort Theater, but after only four nights it closed. Jimmy's performance was the only one which received decent reviews and James Dean the actor, never doubted that he would make it. His relationship with his girlfriend Dizzy Sheridan was now all but over and Jimmy begin a series of brief and meaningless affairs that echoed his inner turmoil. Jimmy was so complex that he never managed to "settle down" with anyone. Because of this, no one ever truly got close to the legend.

Bullfighting was one of Jimmy's obsessions and he visited Mexico several times while living in Hollywood. During one of his jaunts to Mexicali, he met director Budd Boetticher, who was making the movie called "The Bullfighter and The Lady." Boetticher immediately took a liking to Jimmy and gave him a cape which had belonged to the legendary Brooklyn born matador Sidney Franklin. It was a special gift which Jimmy always treasured. He even boasted to some friends how he once fought a two-year old bull, evidence of his compulsive need to sound macho.

To call 1953 a busy year in the career of James Dean is an understatement. His agent had gotten him several roles on TV and he even played Bob Ford in "The Capture of Jesse James," a You Are There! TV drama. Because the two networks were not preserving any of the weekly episodes on film, many of his appearances are only vague memories to those who saw him. Jimmy

played numerous roles, in such memorable series as CBS's Danger, Studio One Summer Theater, NBC's Treasury Men in Action, Campbell Sound Stage, The Big Story, Omnibus, Kraft TV Theater, Armstrong Circle Theater, and Johnson's Wax Program. Many of them are thought to be lost, but some still exist.

The many TV roles that Jimmy landed in 1953 did not keep him away from his wild lifestyle. He acquired an Indian 550 motorbike and traveled around New York; most of the time with a beautiful girl clinging to his waist. Jimmy was also complex and he often found time to read books with which he would impress people with the contents. Some of his favorite hangouts were in Greenwich Village, including trendy spots such as the Louis Tavern, and the San Remo, where he would outwit other actors with his intense mind games.

James Dean was twenty-three years old when the famous Hollywood director Elia Kazan signed him to play Cal Trask in "East of Eden." On April 7, 1954 Jimmy signed a contract with Warner Brothers and received an advance of $700. By the middle of May he bought his first sports car, a used MGTA, and on May 27 shooting began on "East of Eden" in Mendocino, California. Early June saw the film's location shift to Salinas Valley where Steinbeck's novel was actually set. This is where the famous icehouse sequence and the scenes 'out on the land' around Adam Trask's farm were shot.

"East of Eden" was completed on August 13, 1954 and when Steinbeck was introduced to Jimmy for the first time he stated "Jesus Christ, he is Cal!" This prophetic statement was echoed by all who knew Jimmy. His old teachers remarked that Cal Trask was an extension of the boy they knew as James Dean including everything from the funny laugh to his sudden change from frivolity to gloom. The hypnotic aura that James Dean portrays as he prowls the streets of Monterey in the first moments of "East of Eden" was just the beginning of a consummate performance.

Elia Kazan, the director of Jimmy's first major motion picture "East of Eden," had worked before with another unique actor by the name of Marlon Brando. Even though he directed "On The Waterfront," "Viva Zapata" and "A Streetcar Named Desire," it was Kazan's job to convince the studio heads at Warner Brothers to cast an unknown as the lead in a major motion picture. To do this Kazan had made a series of highly suggestive screen tests of Jimmy. The resulting images of an arrogant, angelic, wholesome, and disturbing screen presence was unlike any Kazan had ever witnessed; he had his leading man and the studio heads agreed.

The film "East of Eden" was unique in many ways and not only showcased the talents of Jimmy, but was actually the first half of "Rebel Without a Cause." While this analysis has seldom been discussed. Cal Trask, the character Jimmy so effortlessly portrayed, was a forerunner of Jim Stark the "rebel" Jimmy is most usually associated with. In "East of Eden," James Dean's almost hypnotic performance made teenagers defiantly visible for the first time. It was not so much what Cal said or did that made him unforgettable... but simply what he was! Those who experienced the performance related immediately to their newfound idol.

The two actors that James Dean admired most were originally cast for Jimmy's first leading role in "East of Eden." Both Marlon Brando and Montgomery Cliff could not come to terms with the director, Elia Kazan, and the project was put on hold for a year and a half. However, when the picture was filmed, it used what is known as the CinemaScope process. Movie purists later agreed that with all the wide screen, panoramic scenes and picturesque backgrounds, the CinemaScope process allowed for a more compounded view of the world and enabled the strong psychological presence of Cal Trask to maintain the theme.

During the shooting of "East of Eden" another film was being produced on the Warner Brothers enormous lot. "The Silver Chalice" was the other

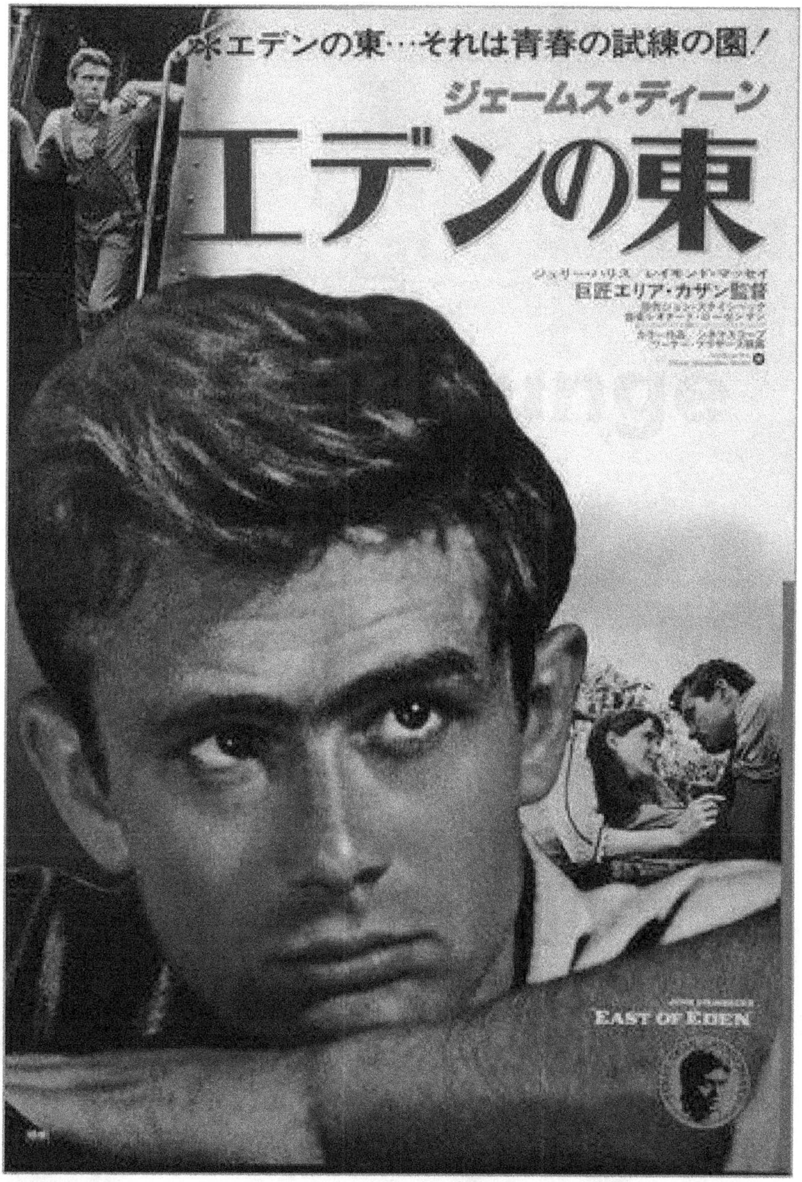
※エデンの東…それは青春の試練の園！
ジェームス・ディーン
エデンの東
巨匠エリア・カザン監督
EAST OF EDEN

film, and it held one more irony in Jimmy's life. The studio originally wanted Jimmy to screen test for the role of the youth who made the "chalice for the last supper." The movie's star, Paul Newman, was a rival of Jimmy's while he lived in New York and had also tested for "East of Eden." In addition, Pier Angeli, the beautiful, young Italian actress, starred in "The Silver Chalice" and later caught the eye of James Dean.

While there were always girls around Jimmy, it was the innocent and beautiful starlet Pier Angeli who truly captured his heart. During a late night break while shooting "East of Eden," Jimmy met Pier, who was with Paul Newman and producer Joseph Wiseman. It was most likely her wholesomeness rather than her beauty which immediately knocked Jimmy off his feet. When Jimmy looked into Pier Angeli's eyes for the first time, the term love at first sight described how he felt that first night. She was a true Italian beauty with a madonna-like face and Jimmy fell in love for the first and only time in his life.

James Dean and Pier Angeli soon became a hot topic in the movie magazines, and to his associates it was clear Jimmy was in love. His outlandish and unpredictable behavior became curbed during this period of his life with Pier. Instead, it was now walks in the moonlight on California beaches which occupied Jimmy's free time. Because Pier's mother would never let her daughter marry a non-Catholic, Pier broke Jimmy's heart and married Vic Damone. On her wedding day, the 'old' Jimmy sat outside the church on his motorcycle and revved the engine as she exited the church.

The "Night Watch" was the name of a group of Jimmy's cronies who met every midnight at Googie's Coffee Bar on Sunset Strip. Now that Pier Angeli was out of his life, Jimmy once again became reckless as well as the focal point of this "crew of creeps," as one gossip writer described them. An unlikely, bizarre figure named Vampira was also a member of this clique. She dressed and looked like a female vampire, complete with straight long black hair and outlandish makeup. This was now the crowd that Jimmy was associating with.

On January 4, 1955, Warner Brothers announced Jimmy would play the role of Jim Stark in "Rebel Without a Cause " which was scheduled to begin shooting on March 28, 1955. However, before that date, Jimmy managed to return home in February with Life magazine photographer Dennis Stock to visit the Winslow and Dean families and to attend the Sweetheart Ball at Fairmount High School. On March 1, 1955 he purchased a 1500 CC Porsche Super Speedster. He would go on to win races at Bakersfield and Pasadena and later entered a two-day meet at Palm Springs.

With the prospect of starring in his second major motion picture in only a few weeks, Jimmy decided to skip the preview of "East of Eden" in New York. The audience at this premiere was filled with stars and Marilyn Monroe even handed out programs. Everyone was there except for Jimmy. Instead he had returned to Hollywood the day before and read about the mostly rave reviews in the newspapers. The director Elia Kazan witnessed a more telling kind of review when teenagers began screaming for Jimmy during another Hollywood preview...not since Sinatra had he witnessed such hysteria.

By the end of March 1955, when shooting began on "Rebel Without a Cause", "East of Eden" had become the number one grossing film in America. The headline on the Fairmount News read "Ex-farmboy now making hay in movies." The mid-50's were strange years in the United States and rock & roll was taking hold of the youth while most teenagers were desperately seeking an idol. "Rebel Without a Cause" had all the ingredients and more significantly it had James Dean who became Jim Stark, the rebel, the idol of millions.

"Rebel Without a Cause", the movie most associated with James Dean, has not been eclipsed by any other movie since in dealing with the psychological troubles of youth. The film's director, Nicholas Ray, intended

to shoot a film about adolescence as seen through the eyes of an adolescent. Jimmy was able to accomplish this and he moved the audience immediately as the first scene of Jim Stark flashed on the big screen. He was a deeply troubled youth with his clothes in disarray, huddled in a small ball on the pavement of a street while playing with a toy monkey as the title flashed on the screen in big bright red letters.

No matter how many times you watch the opening scene of "Rebel," the total charisma and pure performance of Jimmy is overwhelming. He managed to cover the spectrum of emotional looks and feelings with a relaxed style that the viewer can relate to with intense concentration. In one scene Jimmy managed to take a wild swing at a detective during their first encounter, however a few moments later the two were laughing. Jim Stark, the rebel, left the police station as a character you can't wait to follow and see what lies ahead for him.

"Rebel" was planned to be a film about adolescence viewed from within. This theme is carried throughout the film and most feel that without Jimmy in the role of Jim Stark, "Rebel" would have been nothing more than another 50's B movie. The director Nicholas Ray also went to great lengths to add special touches that made the movie even more unique. For example, Natalie Wood's red coat in the opening scene and Jimmy's red trademark jacket and blue jeans were actually over saturated with color. These intricate details along with Jimmy's ability to experience things for the first time, every time made the movie a classic.

"Rebel Without a Cause" takes place in a 24 hour period. Because so much happened, along with Jimmy's presence, one day in the life of Jim Stark captured a lifetime of experiences for the average youth. Who could forget Jim Stark's first day at the new high school, his knife fight, the chickie run, his confrontation with his bickering parents, the midnight rendezvous with Natalie Wood and Sal Mineo, or the planetarium. When Jim Stark drank

理由なき反抗
ジェイムス・ディーン主演
ナタリイ・ウッド サル・ミネオ
ジム・バッカス アン・ドーラン共演
若き世代の痛ましき反抗を描く!!
CINEMASCOPE
製作 ディヴィッド・ウィズバート 原作・監督 ニコラス・レイ
脚色 ステュアート・スターン 音楽 レオナード・ローゼンマン
文部省選定（成人向）優秀映画鑑賞会推薦
ワーナー・ブラザース映画 配給

from a bottle of milk, it touched every adolescent whoever defied their parents' wishes to use a glass.

Unlike most of today stars, Jimmy had much more responsibility in both the development of his character, Jim Stark, and in the total improvisation of each scene. Jimmy's presence was so powerful on the set of "Rebel" that the supporting cast was drawn to Jim Stark, and this unity was evident in the final product. Because there are no weak moments in "Rebel", the viewer, regardless of age is both understanding and sympathetic to Jim Stark's dilemmas.

When the people you work with in any business agree that you are special, you will most likely be successful. In the case of James Dean, even his first director, Elia Kazan, was impressed with the development and spontaneity of his protege's performance in "Rebel". Jim Backus, who played Jimmy's father in "Rebel", said Jimmy had the greatest control over his body of any actor he'd ever seen. While filming a confrontation scene between father and son, Backus was literally dragged across the room and choked, inadvertently by Jimmy.

The Planetarium in "Rebel Without A Cause" stands out in two major scenes and during the actual filming created some unusual events. Jimmy is late as he enters the Planetarium for the first time and at the exact moment that the lecturer states "A star will appear increasingly bright, increasingly near...", the new student Jim Stark gives his name to the woman taking attendance. Ironically, when the night scenes were being shot at the Griffith Park Planetarium, there were so many spot lights that the switchboards of downtown Los Angeles newspapers were flooded with callers reporting a forest fire.

During the shooting of "Rebel", two more major roles were landed by Jimmy. He was scheduled to play Jett Rink in "Giant" and Warner Brothers announced in mid-April that he would star in "Somebody Up There Likes

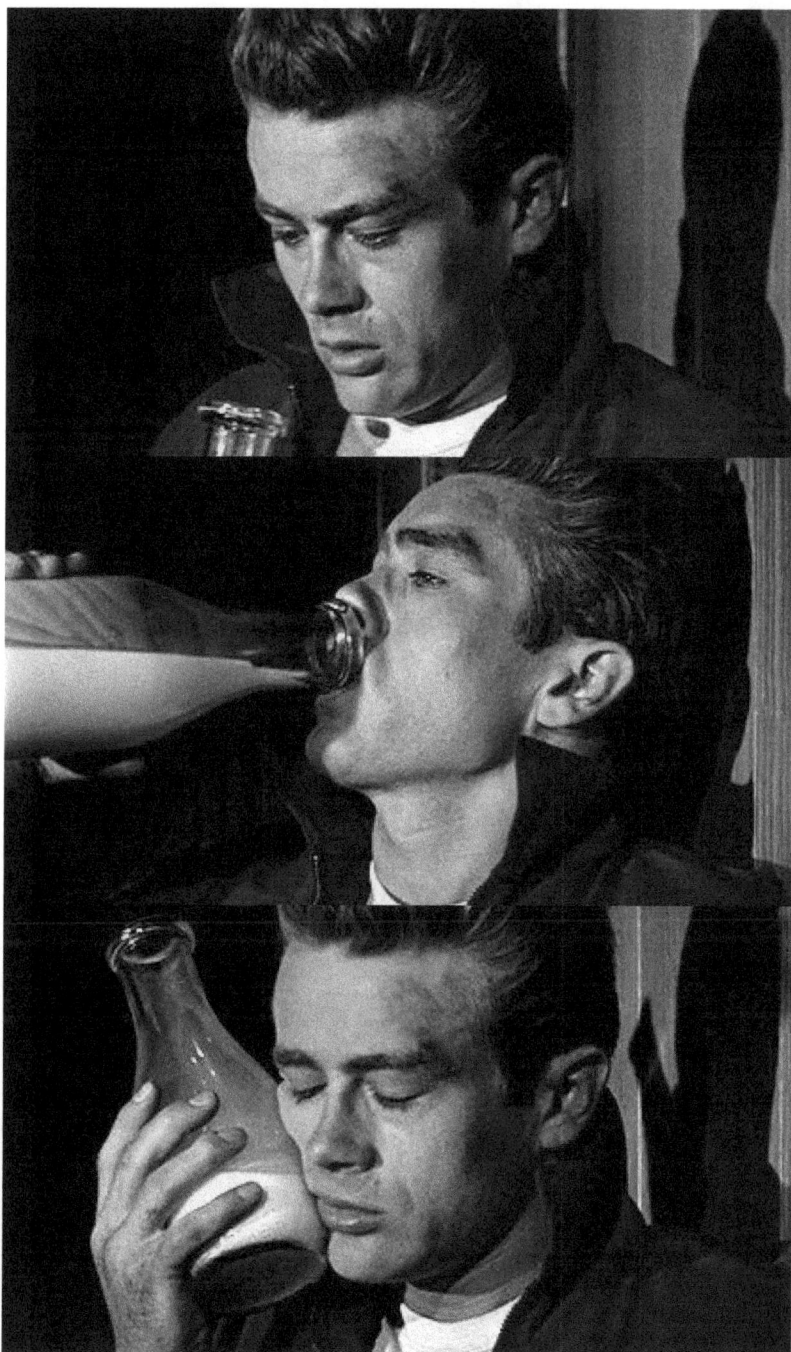

Me." It was evident that the inner circle at Warner Brothers knew how valuable a property James Dean was when they extended his contract. The James Dean mystique was not only taking over the movie-going public--it was taking over the people who ran the movie industry as well.

It is told that Jimmy, Natalie Wood and Sal Mineo, the three long lost souls that came together in "Rebel" as a symbolic father, mother and child, were as close off screen as the characters they portrayed. Natalie Wood summarized Jimmy when she stated, "He was so inspiring, always so patient and kind. He didn't act as if he was a star at all. We all gave each other suggestions, and he was very critical of himself, never satisfied with his work, worried about how every scene would turn out. He was so great when he played a scene, he had the ability to make everyone else look great too."

The dedication that Jimmy displayed while making "Rebel" is evident when you watch the film today, some thirty-seven years since its release. Jimmy began spending less time with his Nightwatch group of friends and even spent less time chasing women. However, his obsession with speed in the form of sport cars had caught the attention of the studio executives who were not happy about Jimmy risking his life on the racetrack. The producers of "Rebel" actually got an assurance from him that he wouldn't race during the making of "Rebel."

There was always a mystical aura that surrounded "Rebel Without A Cause" but unlike other bad luck Hollywood stories, this one was quite unique. Jimmy died tragically in a car accident before the movie actually opened. In addition, two of the other leading characters, Natalie Wood and Sal Mineo, met untimely deaths. Natalie drowned of Catalina Island and Mineo was stabbed to death outside his West Hollywood apartment house. Nick Adams, a friend of Jimmy and fellow gang member in "Rebel" died of a barbiturates overdose and the director Nick Ray died at a young age of cancer.

Upon completion of filming "Rebel" on May 25, 1955, Jimmy couldn't wait to get back on the racetrack and just three days later was racing his Porsche in Santa Barbara, California. His next movie, "Giant" had actually begun filming on May 21, 1955, and Jimmy joined the cast on June 3rd. Jimmy now had the chance to complete his own trilogy by playing an all-American anti-hero, a rock 'n' roll cowboy who ends his life as an alcoholic tycoon in the tuxedo. As Jimmy became Cal Trask in "East of Eden," he now transformed himself into Jett Rink who went from rags to riches when his well came in.

Very few people since James Dean have been considered such a consummate professional. One of today's stars who rivals Dean is Robert DeNiro. DeNiro started as a bona fide boxer at the beginning of "Raging Bull", but by the end of the film he physically was transformed into the overweight Jake LaMotta. In "Giant" Jimmy perfected a Texas accent taught himself to rope cattle and hunted jack rabbits at night to make himself the character of Jett Rink. He was a dedicated perfectionist in every sense of the word.

"Giant" director, George Stevens, had a reputation in Hollywood as the undisputed king of the "Epics." His first order of business with "Giant" was to forbid Jimmy from competing in racing competitions. However this request was only the start of a tumultuous relationship between Jimmy and Stevens, whose directing technique involved shooting scenes from every conceivable angle and then spending months editing out miles of excess footage. Jimmy grew to despise this and quickly distanced himself from some members of the cast and crew.

While Jimmy was able to improvise at will in "Eden" and "Rebel," the director of "Giant" was a stern disciplinarian who would not tolerate any changes in the script by Jimmy. He did not allow any spontaneous touches Jimmy added to his part. It's a wonder that so much of Jimmy survived in the

film and ironically the most distinctive parts about his performance in "Giant" are his gestures of distancing himself from other characters, mumbling into his chest and pulling the brim of his Stetson down over his eyes.

As the filming of "Giant" continued, Jimmy complained endlessly about the director, George Stevens, abuse of his talents. At one point Jimmy was called to work day after day and did nothing more than sit around while Rock Hudson filmed love scenes with Elizabeth Taylor. Finally he decided to take a day off and spent the entire day moving into an apartment he rented in Sherman Oaks. This apartment at 14611 Sutton Street became the Hollywood equivalent of Jimmy's pad in New York. It was designed like a hunting lodge and Jimmy filled it with bizarre objects like a huge bronze eagle, a white bearskin rug, two tape machines and his usual quota of bongos. It was usually noisy long into the night.

Jimmy clearly overshadowed everyone and everything in "Giant". From his first appearance with the ever present Chesterfield in the corner of his mouth and looking like some apprentice of Clint Eastwood, he was the James Dean who simultaneously pushed people away and wanted boyishly to be loved by them. He is the same awkward, seemingly bashful boy with Elizabeth Taylor as he was with Julie Harris and Natalie Wood in his first two films. In one scene of "Giant" when Taylor drops in on him at his meager shack, Jimmy appears more vulnerable and lovable than ever, but this image is lost the second he strikes oil and stands doused in black liquid.

In "Giant" Jimmy's chameleon like characterization of Jett Rink is a litany of Hollywood western types, a virtual tribute to all the great western heroes who came before him. Fittingly when Marlon Brando interpreted the character of Vito Corleone in "The Godfather" he used Jimmy's portrayal of the power crazed oil baron as the basis for his characterization. Brando even incorporated such physical attributes of Jett Rink as the pencil thin mustache and slick black hairstyle in his Vito Corleone persona.

When "Giant" was finally finished, it ran 201 minutes and it became an epic. Besides James Dean, the movie probably contained some of the best work of both Elizabeth Taylor and Rock Hudson. Sal Mineo was also in "Giant" and as in "Rebel" he dies. This 201 minute movie does not drag, it virtually became a showcase for the many talents of James Dean. It was hard to watch the visual images Jimmy portrays in "Giant" without being deeply moved.

At the end of "Giant" it was fate perhaps that allowed Jimmy's fans to actually see the transformation of Jimmy from a young Jett Rink to the pathetic greying old man at the last supper scene. While Rock Hudson and Liz Taylor were excellent in "Giant", their transformation at the end of the movie seemed as if only their hair was gray or that they put on a little weight. Only Jimmy managed to totally transform his character into an old Jett Rink.

On September 21, 1955, Jimmy traded in his Porsche Speedster for a Porsche Spyder 550 and had renowned car customizer George Barris paint the number 130 and "Little Bastard" on the car. September 22, 1955 was the last day Jimmy filmed on "Giant". He planned to race his new car in Salinas between L. A. and San Francisco and on September 30, 1955 he departed with his mechanic Rolf Wutherich and headed for Salinas. At 5:45 PM at the intersection of Routes 466 and 41 near Chalame, his Porsche collided with a Ford sedan. Wutherich was thrown free; Jimmy died within seconds... The legend was born.

JAMES DEAN

JAMES DEAN

JAMES DEAN

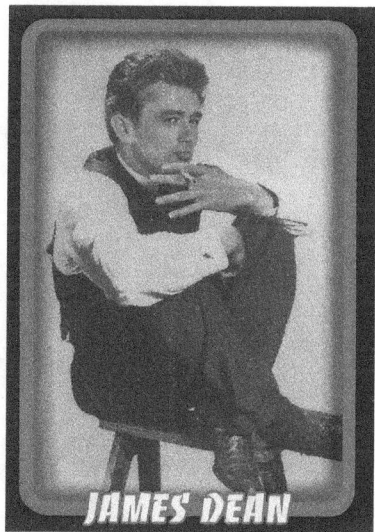

JAMES DEAN

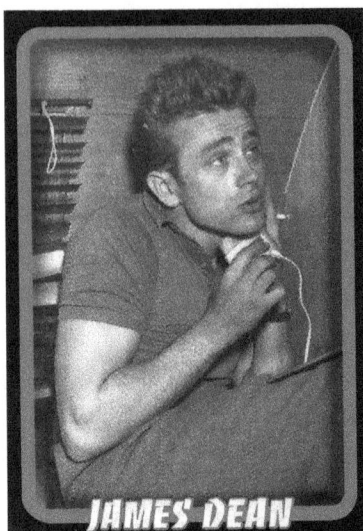

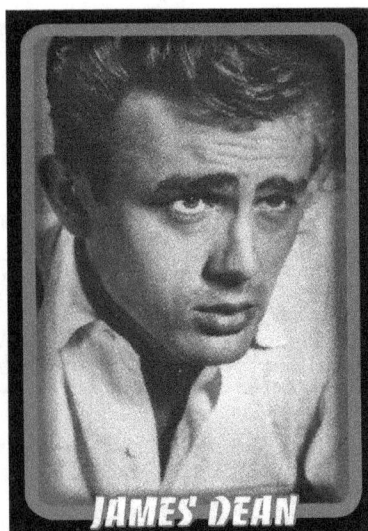

JAMES DEAN

JAMES DEAN

JAMES DEAN

JAMES DEAN

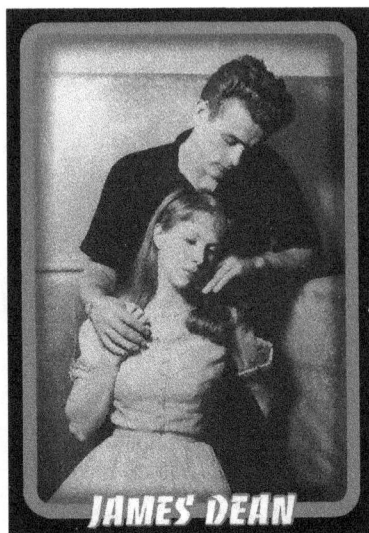

JAMES DEAN

JAMES DEAN

JAMES DEAN

JAMES DEAN

JAMES DEAN

JAMES DEAN

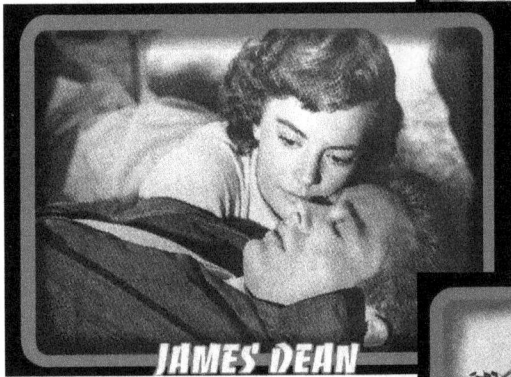

JAMES DEAN

JAMES DEAN

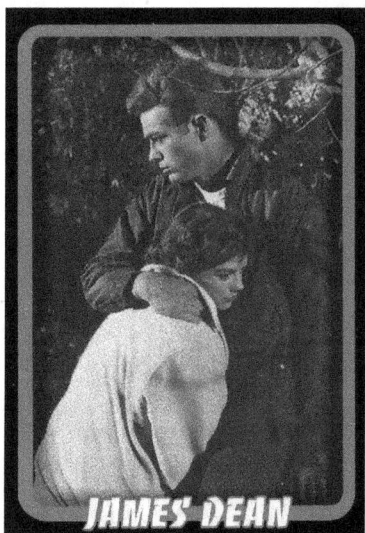

JAMES DEAN

Even though Cal Trask, Jim Stark, and Jett Rink were the only three leading characters James Dean ever portrayed on the big screen, each personality he created stands alone as a definitive work of art. The story of James Dean's life can best be told by drawing from these roles and relating them to incidents surrounding his powerful influence on everyone that he came into contact with, both on and off the screen. James Byron Dean was born February 8, 1931, at 2 AM in the Seven Gables Apartments, 320 East 4th Street, Marion, Indiana....The story begins.

CHAPTER 10

The James Dean Gallery

THERE IS A VERY UNIQUE and special place you must add to your bucket list. Even if you are not a fan of James Dean that special place is The James Dean Gallery. It is located in Fairmount, Indiana. Fairmount Indiana was settled in the 1830s mostly by Quakers from North Carolina. The town was laid out in 1850 and named for Fairmount Park in Philadelphia and it was formally incorporated in 1870. Most of Fairmount was farmland and even today it has a unique and warm feeling of transporting you back to an old time movie. The first time you drive down one of the tree lined streets you will smell the clean fresh air and marvel at the magnificent Victorian houses. The entire town of Fairmount has a little under 3,000 residents. A long time ago in the 1940s to be exact James Dean lived on one of those farms with his aunt and uncle, Ortense and Marcus Winslow. Today one of those magnificent Victorian houses is home to The James Dean Gallery. It is a fitting memorial

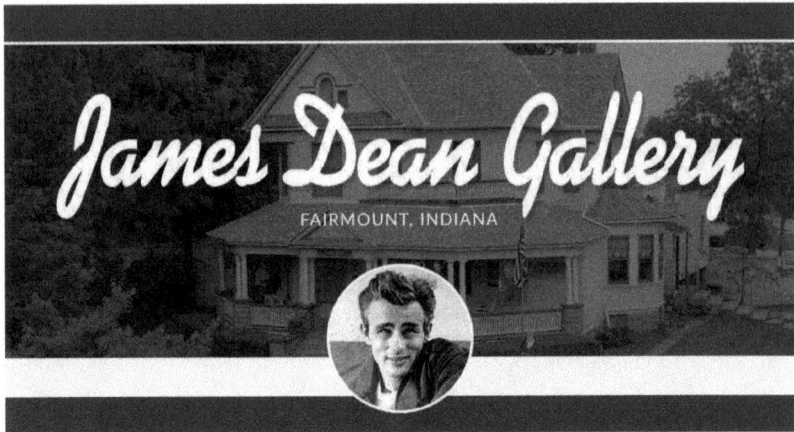

to Jimmy who was just a small town boy who grew up in a place that seems to be frozen in time. When you visit the James Dean Gallery for the first time you might even get a sense that somehow you were there one another time. The only explanation regarding that is because the way the place is set up will remind you of one of Jimmy's movies.

The James Dean Gallery was established in 1988 in the actor's hometown and final resting place of Fairmount, Indiana. This extensive exhibit is the private collection of James Dean archivist David Loehr, who began collecting in 1974. The collection is housed in a beautifully restored 1903 Victorian home, located on tree-lined North Main Street in downtown Fairmount.

The exhibit consists of literally thousands of items of James Dean memorabilia and gives visitors the opportunity to see the worldwide impact that this Indiana native and American film star has made.

As you tour through the exhibit, you'll see childhood photos, high school yearbooks, personal items of James Dean's, along with several dozen original movie posters in several different languages from around the world which show the actor's international impact. There are also books and magazines dedicated to Dean dating from the mid-fifties to the present which are also from many different countries.

The Kenneth Kendall Room features paintings, drawings and sculptures done by the Hollywood artist who created the bronze busts of Dean that are erected at The Griffith Observatory in Los Angeles and at the James Dean Memorial Park in Fairmount.

There are showcases full of tribute and novelty items that have been produced since the 1950s, such as souvenir plates, mugs, ceramic busts, puzzles, gum cards, scarves, and much more.

The archive and library at the gallery has been used by several authors and film-makers working on documentaries and includes over 1,000 photographs, hundreds of books and magazines, and file cabinets full of clippings and information regarding James Dean from birth to death and beyond.

The James Dean Gallery gives visitors an opportunity to view many of the items which have helped to keep the memory of this famous Indiana native alive. There are areas dedicated to "East of Eden", "Rebel Without A Cause " and "Giant". Some of the very unique items are actual clothes that Jimmy wore during the filming of those movies.

Kenneth Kendall Room is dedicated to the Hollywood artist who has immortalized Dean in dozens of paintings, drawings, bronze busts, and statues.

In 1955, James Dean went to the studio of the artist, and requested that Kendall do a bust of him. On the night that James Dean was killed, Mr. Kendall began the sculpture which is now the bronze bust that is erected at both the Griffith Observatory in Los Angeles and at the James Dean Memorial Park in Fairmount. The original small scale model and the full scale model are on display in the Memorial Gallery along with over 50 other pieces of Dean-related art done by Kendall over the years.

The Adeline Nall Room is dedicated to James Dean's high school speech and drama teacher. The room includes showcases dedicated to Dean's three major films, copies of his high school yearbooks, early schoolwork and snapshots from his high school years.

Many people don't realize that besides being a great actor, James Dean was also a very talented artist. Examples of his art are on display in The Adeline Nall Room.

There is also an area called The Novelty Room. There are dozens of commemorative plates and mugs on display in the Novelty Room, along with several different watches and clocks with Dean's image on them.

The James Dean Gallery would not be complete without The Screening Room. In the Screening Room you can relax and watch film clips from several of James Dean's early television dramas, rare screen tests, and an early interview.

The archive and library has been used by several authors and film-makers working on documentaries, and includes over 1,000 photographs, hundreds of books and magazines, and file cabinets full of clippings and information regarding James Dean from birth to death and beyond.

Writer, scholars, and others interested in using the archives are welcome to contact David Loehr for more information.

A visit to The James Dean Gallery would not be complete without taking home some hard to find souvenirs. REBEL REBEL Collectibles is located in the back two rooms of the James Dean Gallery and features a large assortment of 1950's and 1960's Collectibles including lamps, ashtrays, ceramics, books, magazines and other interesting items for sale. The shop is operated by LENNY who also offers his custom handmade Men's button up shirts.

The James Dean Gallery hosts many annual events honoring James Dean. To obtain the exact date each year please visit the website at: www. jamesdeangallery.com

Gallery owner and archivist David Loehr grew up on a farm in Western Massachusetts, studied graphic design at Parson's School of Design in New York, and attended the Lester Polokov School for Stage Design.

In 1974 a friend gave him the book, James Dean: The Mutant King by David Dalton. David read the book while travelling from New York to California, where he lived for five years in Pasadena. While in California, he saw all three of Dean's major films on the big screen for the first time, and was knocked out by Dean's performances.

He picked up another book, a poster, a magazine, and before he knew it, he was collecting James Dean memorabilia. This has now become the world's

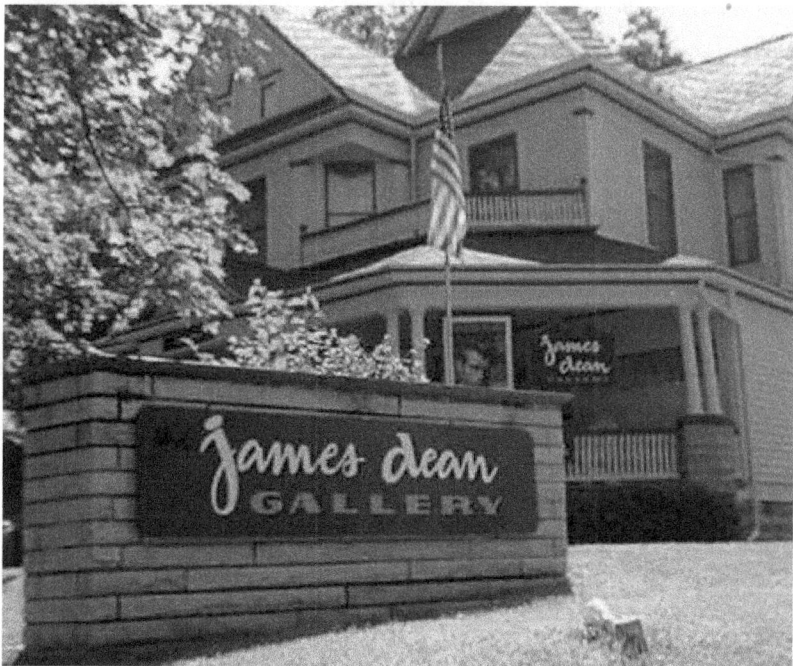

largest collection of Dean memorabilia; and what was a small hobby has turned into a full time job and career.

In 1982, David conducted the First Annual Walking Tour of James Dean's New York Hangouts, which lasted 6 hours and visited over 30 points of interest from Dean's early days in the city. He continued the annual tours for the next ten years.

In 1988, after dozens of trips to Fairmount spanning 14 years, David opened the James Dean Gallery to the public for the first time. Since then, it has continued to grow in popularity, and now attracts tens of thousands of visitors each year and is one of Grant County's most popular tourist attractions.

Over the years, David has worked on dozens of James Dean projects including books such as: James Dean: American Icon, James Dean: Shooting Star, James Dean: Tribute to a Rebel, and The Official James Dean Book. He has also contributed to several documentaries, including James Dean: Forever Young, Forever James Dean, James Dean: a Portrait, James Dean and Me, Born Cool, and several foreign documentaries.

David and the James Dean Gallery have been featured on numerous television shows, including: A Current Affair, 20/20, To Tell the Truth, Entertainment Tonight, The Joe Franklin Show, New York Profiles, Across Indiana, Strange Universe, The Good Night Show, many local television news shows, and a live, in studio appearance on a popular Japanese television show.

David currently publishes a quarterly James Dean Gallery Newsletter and continues to operate the Museum Exhibit and Gift Shop in Fairmount.

Sample copy of newsletter

CHAPTER 11

Interesting Facts
and Observations

Elia Kazan was not only a producer and director, but also a writer and actor. The prestigious New York Times described him as "one of the most honored and influential directors in Broadway and Hollywood history". He co-founded the Actors Studio. The Studio is credited with introducing "Method Acting" under the direction of Lee Strasberg. An indication of how great a director and producer Kazan was, is how he was able to get the best dramatic performances from all of his actors. Elia directed 21 actors to Oscar nominations, resulting in nine wins. He directed a string of successful films, including *A Streetcar Named Desire* (1951), *On the Waterfront* (1954), and *East of Eden* (1955). During his career, he won two Oscars as Best Director and received an Honorary Oscar, won three Tony Awards, and four

Golden Globes. The two Oscars he won were for Best Director, *Gentleman's Agreement* (1948), and *On the Waterfront* (1955). He was the first director to work with James Dean and he recognized how gifted he was.

Another great Hollywood director also worked with James Dean. Following is how George Stevens handled Jimmy during the filming of *Giant* after they had a major disagreement. He decided that for the rest of the movie shoot he told the cameramen to just keep the cameras rolling. He wanted to get as much unrehearsed footage of Jimmy as he could. George saw how great the spontaneous everyday actions of Jimmy were.

It turned out to be the right decision on his part, because for all his innovative techniques regarding the way he directed actors in the past, in many ways even he was surprised. George's gamble was correct. It brought him the reward that every director seeks. The challenge of this bright new actor, it paid off. George won the Oscar for Best Director. A scene that defines the movie, the cinematography complete with a music score and no dialog is the first time Jimmy checks out his inherited piece of land. There he is in the vastness of a Texas wasteland with an old wire fence just taking large steps. He is decked out in his cowboy hat, dirty jeans, a vest and is pacing off the land, almost like he is measuring it. In his hand is a paper, must be the deed, the sky is vast and covered in puffy white clouds. He comes to a section of the fence and makes a slight adjustment to the wire or post. He is saying with his actions, I own this now! He continues walking and kicks an old tin bucket, walks a little more, then removes his hat and places it on the top of a fence post. He gazes out to the vast horizon and then begins to take those long measuring steps, all the while the music is complementing the scene. Suddenly he approaches an old wind mill, he pauses and begins to climb up it. Jimmy reaches a platform near the top, appears to be mesmerized and as he sits down with his legs dangling he gently folds his arms and gazes down. The camera switches to the land below. Jimmy is telling the world, not with words but with his actions. I came from nothing but now I have something that one day will make me great.

Jimmy could have been one of the *Wild Bunch* or most likely *The*

Magnificent Seven. When you finish watching any one of the three James Dean movies your creative mind begins to wander. Maybe you get the same sensations after watching some of his television performances. Of course it might be because you admire his outstanding way of approaching every role and character he took on. However, in the case of James Dean there is much more that can be said about the old adage of "what might have been". The decades that followed after the untimely death of James Dean were filled with countless classic movies. Within those movies were some of the most unique and memorable characters ever to grace the big screen. Keep in mind Jimmy was only twenty-four years old when he left us. Another great actor comes to mind when imagining Jimmy in some of his roles that are thought of as great and interesting. That actor is Al Pacino. There have been many great actors that come to mind when looking to imagine the roles that James Dean might have played but it is Al Pacino that will be the first to compare. Great actors have that uncanny ability to not only play a character in a movie but more importantly to actually become that character. Marlon Brando was one of the best at evolving into any role that he played. Al Pacino had that gift also and it was manifested in the movie, *Dog Day Afternoon*. On the surface the movie and its main character, a hapless bank robber is not that interesting. The movie in question, *Dog Day Afternoon* was based on a real life incident. In August 1972, first-time crook Sonny Wortzik, played by Pacino and his friend Sal Naturale played by John Cazale attempt to attempt to rob the First Brooklyn Savings Bank. The plan backfires goes when Stevie the third would be bank robber loses his nerve shortly after Sal pulls out his gun. Sonny is forced to let him flee the scene. In the vault, Sonny discovers that he and Sal have arrived after the daily cash pickup, and only $1,100 in cash remains in the bank. What follows is a series of events highlighted by Sal and Sonny deciding to take the bank employees and customers hostage. The movie was well received and Al Pacino was nominated for an Oscar as Best Actor in a leading role. Here is where the argument can be made regarding James Dean. Personally I felt that Pacino should have won but when the winner was announced I was satisfied with the choice. The winner of the

Oscar in 1976 was Jack Nicholson, for *One Flew Over The Cuckoo's Nest*. Once again taking nothing away from Al Pacino's brilliant performance, James Dean might have had just a little more innovative over the top presence to beat out Nicholson. James Dean would have once again much like he did in the opening scene in *Rebel Without A Cause*, captivate the audience with his very compelling demeanor. In regard to his interactions with the bank hostages, Jimmy would have mesmerized all of them especially the woman. His boyish charm coupled with his outrageous mannerisms were absolutely perfect for the role that made everyone take notice of the great Pacino. Since we are discussing Al Pacino and James Dean regarding the comparison of how each approached a specific role, one more Pacino movie comes to mind. The movie is *The Godfather*. Everyone has seen *The Godfather* at least once but most people will admit they have seen it numerous times. When comparing a role that James Dean might have mastered and perhaps portrayed so good that an Oscar was almost guaranteed this is another one. It is not the role Al Pacino had as Michael Corleone but the less thought of role that John Cazale had as Fredo. Before we discuss James Dean and how he might have approached the character Fredo, we must acknowledge the greatness that John Cazale brought to the motion picture industry. John Cazale had the distinction of appearing in only five motion pictures, however all five were nominated for the Best Motion Picture Oscar. The movies are, *The Godfather, The Conversation, The Godfather Part II, Dog Day Afternoon*, and *The Deer Hunter*. He appeared in archival footage in *The Godfather Part III*, also nominated for Best Picture. John is the only actor to have this unique theatrical distinction. He too left us at a young age. John Cazale died in New York City on March 13, 1978, shortly after completing his role in *The Deer Hunter*. He was only forty-two years old. One of the great directors he worked with commented.

"One of the things that I love about the casting of John Cazale was that he had a tremendous sadness about him. I don't know where it came from; I don't believe in invading the privacy of the actors that I work with, or getting into their heads. But, my God — it's there — every shot of him. And not just in this movie, but in *Godfather II* also.» That director was none other

than Sidney Lumet. Jimmy had that distinction of being much more than just an actor reading a script and playing a character. Jimmy much like John Cazale possessed that «it» factor. You can't teach it. You will never be able to master it by practice. It is an intangible characteristic that very few actors possess. Of course James Dean has been compared to Marlon Brando but this comparison between him and John Cazale is special. It is a comparison that when you delve into all the nuances that make it up you will be convinced. If James Dean would have been given the opportunity to cast for one of the sons of Don Corleone, most likely he would have been selected to play Fredo. The role was tailor made for Jimmy. Fredo was the sensitive son but he was the one who was perhaps closest to his father, played by Marlon Brando. It would have been the perfect marriage of two of Hollywood's greatest stars playing a father and a son. The other reason why it would have been a match for James Dean was how complex Fredo was. He was a multi dimensional personality but even though his scenes were limited he was able to make a lasting impact. When you envision the the possibility of James Dean as Don Corleone's most vulnerable son, it is evident you will agree it was one of the roles James Dean would have been perfect for.

In 1969 the third highest grossing motion picture was *Easy Rider*. The movie had a trio of very iconic stars and they would have welcomed James Dean to the cast. The three stars were, Peter Fonda, Dennis Hopper and Jack Nicholson. One of those three stars Dennis Hopper became a close friend of James Dean after Hopper was in two of Dean's movies. He had the distinction of being in both *Rebel Without a Cause* and *Giant*. The movie *Easy Rider* was groundbreaking on many levels and there is no doubt that had Jimmy lived his association with Dennis Hopper would have guaranteed he would have been given a role as perhaps the third biker. The movie was another vehicle for James Dean which would have most definitely given him the opportunity to perhaps win the Oscar he deserved for all of his only three movies.

There was a time when movies were unique and special. The movies were an art form jam packed with creativity. A time long ago when going to see a movie was an enlightening experience. It was a way of getting enjoyment from a media form that asked for nothing in return. If you want to know what it was like I will attempt to describe it and the movies as I remember them. A good opening example is to compare the very first James Bond movie to the current one. *Dr. No,* released in 1962 and the latest Bond movie Spectre, released in 2015. *Dr. No* had its villain and plenty of beautiful girls but the special effects were very limited. In *Dr. No* the only special items were an exploding suitcase and a cyanide cigarette. However in *Spectre* you might be overwhelmed by all the car chases, explosions, high flying feats of daring. Most of the action in *Spectre* was created on a computer. In retrospect the action in *Dr. No* was real. Of course *Dr. No* was just a movie but it was all taking place without the help of a computer. The very first *Godzilla* was released in Japan in 1954, was then released in the United States in 1956. During the next six decades there have been many Godzilla movies all made in Japan. In 1998 a Godzilla movie made in America was released. Then in 2014 a second Hollywood Godzilla movie was released. Getting back to the 1956 Toho production there are many unique factors regarding this very first Japanese Godzilla movie. The producers wanted to use the stop-motion animation technique formulated by Willis O'Brien in the original 1933 King Kong. It was determined that the movie would take about seven years because of all the action scenes they planned. The producers settled on "suitmation" as the best way to complete the movie. It was basically a man in a Godzilla costume. Another interesting fact about the very first *Godzilla* movie is that if you compare it to other black and white films of the 1950's it has a film noir feel to it. Yes, the first *Godzilla* is actually film noir. The antiquated special effects were simply a man in a dinosaur costume destroying miniature buildings complete with pyrotechnics. The strange thing is that it worked but more important is the audience was completely satisfied. It really didn't matter that the man was in a dinosaur costume breaking tiny plastic buildings. By stark contrast the 1998 *Godzilla* was almost entirely made up of special effects that were very over the top. The 1998 movie had a promising beginning and a very good cast but once Godzilla made his appearance the movie was a major disappointment. These examples and

comparisons clearly show the differences between the two era's of movies. All three of James Dean's movies had no special effects and held the viewers interest from the start to finish. James Dean was one of the reasons why you exited the movie theater with a good feeling. An experience that was good because of the performance and the star quality of James Dean. The three movies were also memorable for the supporting cast as well as their story and production values. It was the acting and not some computer generated non-stop action that attracted you. It would be extremely difficult to envision James Dean playing a character in any recent movie. He would even not fit in as a hero or a villain in the current James Bond movies because he was too much of an artist. Another genre of movies that immediately come to mind when explaining the comparison between movies of today as opposed to the 50's and 60's is the pirate movie. It would be hard to imagine James Dean in the role of Captain Jack Sparrow. The early pirate movies made famous by Errol Flynn, Anthony Quinn and Burt Lancaster had virtually no special effects. They relied completely on outstanding acting as well as plenty of real action and magnificent cinematography. The series of *Pirates of the Caribbean* movies had just as many over the top special effects as the James Bond movies. In many ways the entire movie industry is devoid of creativity and lacks the artistic quality of the actors and actresses of the past. Even the classic Universal Monsters have evolved into movies with countless scenes of special effects. The original *Mummy* with Boris Karloff as the star had no special effects. Boris Karloff used his unique personality to convey fear and horror, without any help from computer generated images. By contrast the current *Mummy* movie with Tom Cruise as the leading man relies heavily on special effects. The Tom Cruise *Mummy* pays little or no homage to the original classic and is devoid of any real drama much less horror. The era of movies both before James Dean appeared in his three classic movies had paved the way for creativity. It was the producers, directors, cinematographers, actors and actresses that made them great. That creativity lasted for several more years and then in the 1960's stop motion animation entered the scene with movies like *The Seventh Voyage of Sinbad* and the sequels that followed.

Then in the 1980's the very first *Star Wars* movie opened the door for CGI. It was the beginning of George Lucas visual effects company, Industrial Light and Magic. It was a unique experience for filmgoers who were witnessing modern day special effects for the very first time. Other pioneers of CGI, (computer generated images), James Cameron, Michael Bay, Peter Jackson and Steven Spielberg took the movie experience into a different dimension.

As the winter months begin to fade and spring's freshness breezes against my face, I begin to look toward summer and its warmth. Each and every summer as I have done for over sixty years I plan several trips to exotic locations. The reason why I choose to mention personal thoughts is because for me they have a relevance to James Dean. My journeys began in quaint Cape Cod way back in the early fifties. It was a time of happiness for me and perhaps the entire country. The Cape was a peaceful place with its quaint little villages and of course the ocean. One summer it was 1955 to be exact I went to a drive in movie and one of the features was *Rebel Without a Cause*. The drive in experience was one that today is dearly missed. However back in the 1950's almost every little town had their own drive in theater. The next day as I lay on the sandy beach I was thinking about Jim Stark, Jimmy's character who was etched in my mind from the night before.

As you watch the opening scene in the police station there are many reasons why James Dean should have at the least been nominated for the Oscar. The similarities in his mannerisms as well as his delivery of his lines are exactly as Heath Ledger did over five decades later as the Joker in *The Dark Knight*. Then still at the police station as Jimmy interacts with the police detective he punches the wooden desk exactly like Robert De Niro did in *Raging Bull*. Watch the scene and you will agree even the way De Niro looks at his wounded hands is a mirror image as the way Jimmy looked at his hands.

Rebel without a Cause is a groundbreaking movie and the one that most individuals associate with James Dean. The story begins about disillusioned teen who has just moved to a new town. Jim Stark (James Dean) is supposed get a brand new start after previous encounters forced his family to move. It is suggested but the details were never revealed. While searching new

friends and a desire to fit in, Jim Stark forms a unique bond with a disturbed classmate, Plato (Sal Mineo). Then he falls head over heels for a rich local girl Judy (Natalie Wood). However, Judy is the girlfriend of the leader of a gang of tough guys. His name is Buzz (Corey Allen). There is a confrontation between Jimmy and Buzz that ends up with a drag race. The movie has many sub-plots as well as a host of big name Hollywood stars in supporting roles. The brilliant photography is enhanced by outstanding locations. *Rebel Without a Cause* and it's stars received three Oscar nominations. Natalie Wood was nominated for the Oscar in the Best Supporting Actress category. Sal Mineo was also nominated in the Best Supporting Actor category. The director Nicholas Ray was nominated for Best Writing, Motion Picture Story. Unfortunately, all three did not win an Oscar. This is also the only movie out of the three that James a Dean starred in, that did not get him an Oscar nomination.

On February 19, 1966 Columbia Pictures released a very special melodrama, *The Chase*. The movie was directed by the renowned Arthur Penn and produced by Sam Spiegel. It had quite a cast which included some of Hollywood's biggest stars of the sixties. With names like Marlon Brando, Robert Redford, Jane Fonda, E. G. Marshall, Angie Dickerson, Janice Rule, Robert Duvall and Henry Hull, it should have been a big blockbuster movie. However, for some reason it was not well received and only took in a modest 2.3 million at the box office. The movie was panned by the critics in America but in Europe it was a big hit. Before we get to the details regarding the story it is most definitely a movie that James Dean could have saved. The word saved is used specifically because *The Chase* did not receive one nomination in any category. That included not only the Academy Awards and Golden Globe Awards but each and every other award presentation. The film score was by the renowned John Barry who won numerous Academy Awards, Golden Globes and BAFTA Awards. The same John Barry who composed music scores for eleven of the James Bond movies. James Dean would have been in his mid thirties and the perfect age to take on Robert Redford's role in *The Chase*. The movie was set in a small Texas town and the story follows many unique characters. Marlon Brando is Sheriff Calder a friend of Robert

Redford's character, Charlie "Bubber" Reeves. Jane Fonda is Anna Reeves "Bubber's" wife. The story begins as "Bubber" is escaping from prison and is heading back to his home town to reunite with his wife. Unlike the movies of today The Chase made use of all the supporting characters. Each and every actor nailed his role and the interaction was spectacular. Angie Dickerson played Ruby Calder, Sheriff Calder's wife and her scenes with her husband Brando are quite memorable. Jane Fonda was having an affair with Jake Rogers played expertly by James Fox. His character Jake Rogers and "Bubber" were best friends before "Bubber" was sent to jail. The entire movie centers around the many different characters and most of *The Chase* takes place on one Saturday night. Sheriff Calder has the task of not only bringing "Bubber" back to jail, but protecting him from the angry mob that wants to harm him. In the aftermath Sheriff Calder suffers a very savage beating from the mob. Charlie "Bubber" Reeves was the character that had the potential to make the movie special. Sheriff Calder was played to the hilt by Brando but the interaction between him and "Bubber" lacked any enthusiasm or chemistry. James Dean would relish in the role as "Bubber" he would light up the screen with his mannerisms and total emulsion in the character. Just put Jim Stark and Jett Rink together in one personality and you would have the perfect "Bubber".

There are many different reasons why James Dean most definitely deserves the Oscar. The Oscar has always been a symbol of the culmination of a performance by an actor or an actress that is by far the best of that specific year. Here we are some sixty years since *Giant* was released. Sixty years, that's six decades. It is safe to say that in those six decades not one other actor has come along that you can even slightly compare to Jimmy. He has left a legacy that will endure ten times those first sixty years. The performances in all three of his only motion pictures stand alone. They stand alone as reminders of a unique once in a lifetime experience. If you were fortunate to live in the era when Jimmy's three movies were playing in the big theaters, you know. You can recall the persona of Jimmy and those three men he brought to life as if it were a month or so ago. Which of the three is the best and stands out? That is a very tough question and choice to make. The first one that comes to mind is Jim Stark, in *Rebel Without a Cause*. However, Jett Rink, Jimmy's character in *Giant* is the one that should convince the powers that be to honor this phenomenal performance. The young Jett Rink character has been discussed but what about the old Jett Rink? When the movie culminated into the epic saga that it was all of the main characters had aged over twenty five years. Both Rock Hudson and Elizabeth Taylor were now grandparents and Jett Rink was an old alcoholic oil tycoon. Jimmy really was able to capture the persona of an old man to perfection. His every movement was like it had been filmed in slow motion. He even managed to slur his words. Of course there was makeup used to help visualize the affect. Rock Hudson and Elizabeth Taylor's transformation was enhanced with grey wigs and facial adornments. James Dean's version of the old Jett Rink was more, much more than physical adjustments with makeup. James Dean became and was an old man in every sense of the word.

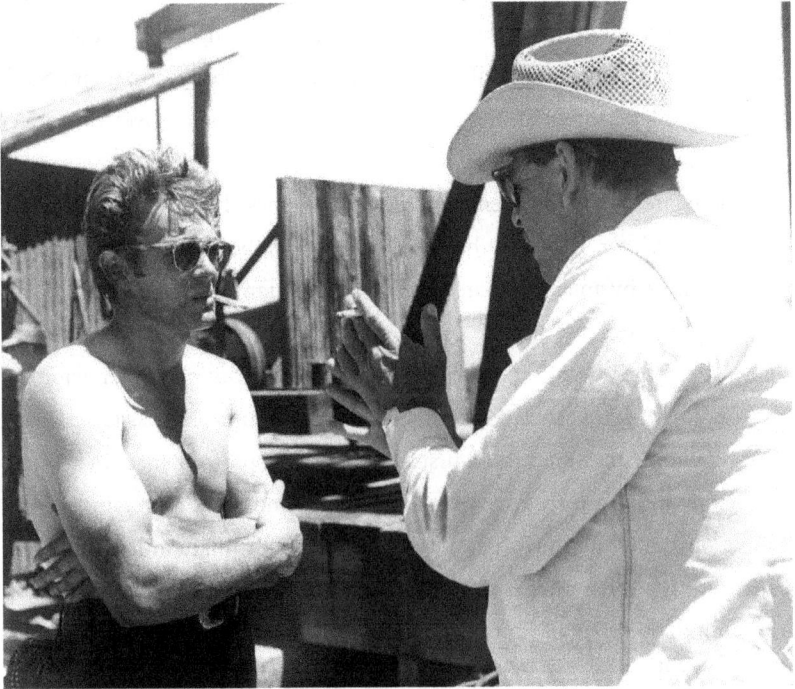

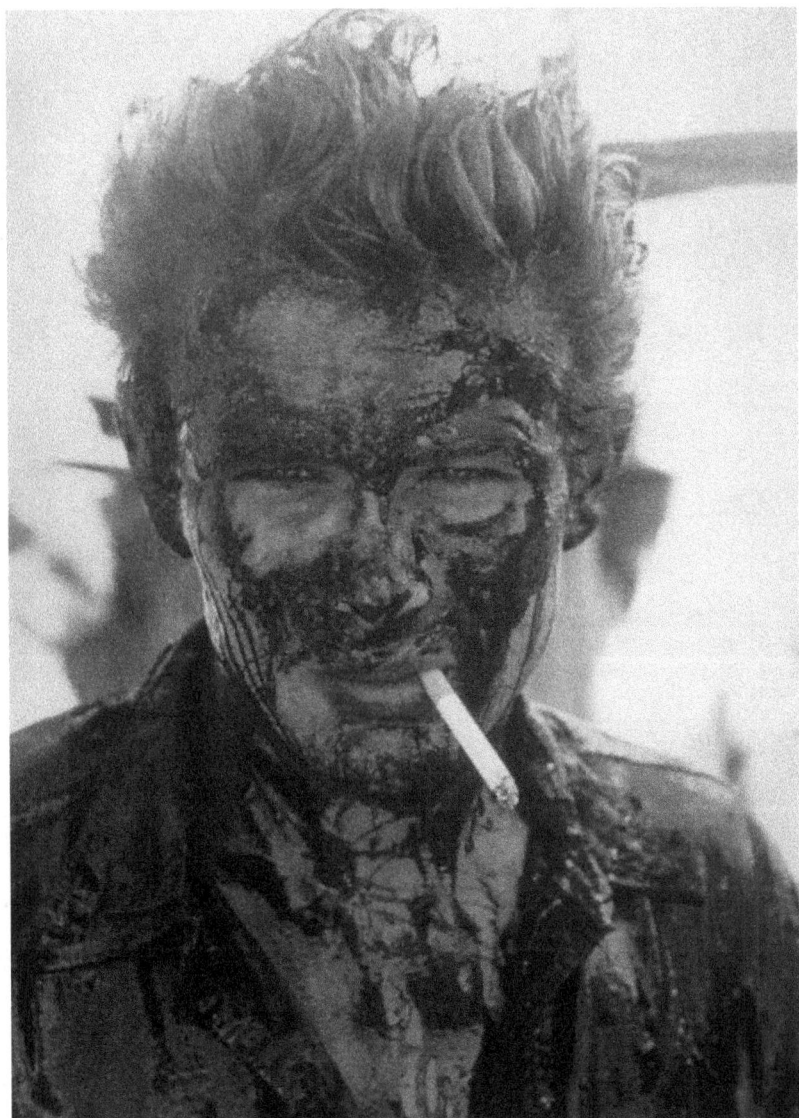

CHAPTER 12

The James Dean Filmography and Television Credits

East of Eden 1955 N/R, 117 Minutes

Genre: Drama
Director: Elia Kazan
Producer: Elia Kazan
Screenplay: Paul Osborn
Cinematography: Ted D. McCord
Soundtrack: Leonard Rosenman
Cast: James Dean, Julie Harris, Raymond Massey
Jo Van Fleet, Burl Ives, Albert Dekker, Richard
Davalos, Lois Smith, Timothy Carey, Harold
Gordon, Nick Dennis, Barbara Baxley

James Dean portrays one of the two sons of a devoutly religious farmer. His character is a moody unique young man who believes his father favors the other son. The movie was based on the best selling John Steinbeck novel East of Eden. The movie takes place mostly in Salinas Valley, California. Steinbeck based the novel on the fourth chapter of Genesis which recounts the story of Cain and Abel. It can be noted that of the three movies that James Dean made this is the only one he actually viewed.

Cast

James Dean..................................Cal Trask
Raymond Massey...........................Adam Trask
Julie Harris....................................Abra Bacon
Richard Davalos............................Aron Trask
Burl Ives.......................................Sam the Sheriff
Jo Van Fleet..................................Cathy Ames/Kate Trask
Albert Dekker...............................Will Hamilton
Lois Smith.....................................Anne, Kate's Servant
Timothy Carey...............................Joe, Kate's Henchman
Harold Gordon..............................Gustav Albrecht
Nick Dennis...................................Rantani
Barbara Baxley..............................Adam's Nurse

Rebel Without a Cause 1955 N/R, 111 Minutes

Genre: Melodrama
Director: Nicholas Ray
Producer: David Weisbart
Screenplay: Stewart Stern, Irving Shulman (adaptation)
Cinematography: Ernest Haller
Soundtrack: Leonard Rosenman
Cast: James Dean, Natalie Wood, Sal Mineo, Jim Backus

Ann Doran, Corey Allen, William Hopper, Rochelle
Hudson, Edward Platt, Dennis Hopper, Frank Mazzola
Nick Adams, Jack Grinnage, Ian Wolfe, Beverly Long
Virginia Brissac, Jack Simmons, Marietta Canty,
Steffi Sidney, John Righetti

James Dean portrays Jim Stark, the rebel in the role in which he
became a 20th century icon. He was not alone in his search for love and
understanding. There are two other dominant characters, one a troubled
female and the other a disillusioned youth. The three find each other
and act like a family. One of the movies additional achievements was the
cinematography. The outdoor scenes were in many ways groundbreaking.
It can also be noted that this is the only one of James Dean's three movies
where he received top billing.

Cast

James Dean..............................Jim Stark
Natalie Wood...........................Judy
Sal Mineo................................John "Plato" Crawford
Jim Backus..............................Frank Stark
Ann Doran...............................Carol Stark
Corey Allen.............................Buzz Gunderson
William Hopper.........................Judy's Father
Rochelle Hudson.......................Judy's Mother
Edward Platt............................Ray Fremick
Dennis Hopper..........................Goon
Nick Adams..............................Chick
Frank Mazzola..........................Crunch
Jack Grinnage..........................Moose
Steffi Sidney...........................Mil

Beverly Long...............................Helen

Virginia Brissac...........................Grandma Stark

Marietta Canty...........................Crawford Family's Maid

Jack Simmons...........................Cookie

John Righetti.............................The Big Rig

Ian Wolfe...................................Astronomy Professor

Giant 1956 N/R, 201 Minutes

Genre: Epic Western Drama

Director: George Stevens

Producers: George Stevens, Henry Ginsberg

Screenplay: Fred Guiol, Ivan Moffat

Cinematography: William C. Mellor

Soundtrack: Dimitri Triokin

Cast: Elizabeth Taylor, Rock Hudson, James Dean, Carroll Baker, Mercedes McCambridge, Chill Wills, Dennis Hopper, Fran Bennett, Paul Fix, Judith Evelyn, Carolyn Craig, Rod Taylor, Sal Mineo, Charles Watts, Maurice Jara, Alexander Scourby, Noreen Nash, Mickey Simpson

James Dean portrays Jett Rink, a cowboy on a sprawling Texas ranch owned by Rock Hudson. Jimmy manages to add unique realism to the Rink character by going from a young ranch hand, then to an old oil baron. The epic production was based on the best selling novel, "Giant", by Edna Ferber. It covers all aspects of Texas prosperity spanning two generations. Keep in mind Jimmy was only twenty-four years old yet managed to convince the audience he was the old man Jett Rink. It was his second

Academy Award nomination.

Cast

Elizabeth Taylor.............................Leslie Lynnton Benedict

Rock Hudson................................Jordan "Bick" Benedict Jr.

James Dean...................................Jett Rink

Carroll Baker...............................Luz Benedict ll, (Bick's daughter)

Mercedes McCambridge................Luz Benedict, (Bick's sister)

Chill Wills.....................................Uncle Bawley

Dennis Hopper.............................Jordon "Jordy" Benedict lll

Fran Bennett.................................Judy Benedict

Paul Fix...Dr. Horace Lynnton

Judith Evelyn................................Mrs. Nancy Lynnton

Carolyn Craig...............................Lacy Lynnton

Rod Taylor....................................Sir David Karfrey

Sal Mineo.....................................Angel Obregon ll

Charles Watts...............................Judge Oliver Whiteside

Maurice Jara.................................Dr. Guerra

Alexander Scourby........................Old Polo

Noreen Nash................................Lola Lane

Mickey Simpson...........................Sarge, owner of Sarge's diner

James Dean early film appearances:

Fixed Bayonets! 1951
Uncredited role as a soldier named Doggie

Sailor Beware 1952
Uncredited role as Jerry Lewis' boxing opponent's second

Has Anybody Seen My Gal 1952
Uncredited role as the youth at soda fountain

Deadline-USA 1952
Uncredited role as a copy boy

Trouble Along the Way 1953
Uncredited extra in crowd at a football game

JAMES DEAN TELEVISION APPEARANCES

Studio One in Hollywood (1948)
Episode Title: Ten Thousand Horses Singing
Role: Hotel Bellboy

Studio One in Hollywood (1948)
Episode Title: Abraham Lincoln
Role: William Scott

Studio One in Hollywood (1948)
Episode Title: Sentence of Death
Role: Joe Palica

The Big Story (1949)
Episode Title: Rex Newman, Reporter for the Globe and News
Role: Rex Newman

Family Theater (1949)
Episode Title: Hill Number One, A Story of Faith and Inspiration
Role: St. John the Apostle

The Bigelow Theater (1950)
Episode Title: T.K.O.
Role: Hank

The Stu Erwin Show (1950)
Episode Title: Jackie Knows All
Role: Randy

CBS Television Workshop (1952)
Episode Title: Into the Valley
Role: G.I.

The Web (1950)
Episode Title: Sleeping Dogs
Role: Himself

Hallmark Hall of Fame (1951)
Episode Title: The Forgotten Children
Role: Bradford

The Kate Smith Hour (1950)
Episode Title: The Hound of Heaven
Role: The Messenger

You Are There (1953)
Episode Title: The Capture of Jesse James
Role: Bob Ford

Treasury Men in Action (1950)
Episode Title: The Case of the Sawed-Off Shotgun
Role: Arbie Ferris

Treasury Men in Action (1950)
Episode Title: The Case of the Watchful Dog
Role: Randy Meeker

Tales of Tomorrow (1951)
Episode Title: The Evil Within
Role: Ralph

Omnibus (1952)
Episode Title: Glory in the Flower
Role: Bronco Evans

Campbell Summer Soundstage (1952)
Episode Title: Life Sentence
Role: Hank Brandon

Campbell Summer Soundstage (1952)
Episode Title: Something for an Empty Briefcase
Role: Joe

Kraft Theater (1952)
Episode Title: A Long Time Till Dawn
Role: Joe Harris

Kraft Theater (1952)
Episode Title: Keep Our Honor Bright
Role: Jim

Armstrong Circle Theater (1953)
Episode Title: The Bells of Cockaigne
Role: Joey Frazier

Robert Montgomery Presents (1953)
Episode Title: Harvest
Role: Paul Zalinka

The Philco-Goodyear Television Playhouse (1954)
Episode Title: Run Like a Thief
Role: Rob

Danger (1953)
Episode Title: Padlocks
Role: Felon

Danger (1953)
Episode Title: The Little Woman
Role: Augie

Danger (1953)
Episode Title: Death is my Neighbor
Role: J.. B.

Danger (1953)
Episode Title: No Room
Role: Himself

General Electric Theater (1953)
Episode Title: The Dark, Dark Hours
Role: Bud

General Electric Theater (1953)
Episode Title: I'm a Fool
Role: The Boy

The United States Steel Hour (1953)
Episode Title: The Thief
Role: Fernand Lagarde

Lux Video Theater (1952)
Episode Title: The Foggy, Foggy Dew
Role: Kyle McCallum

Lux Video Theater (1952)
Episode Title: The Life of Emile Zola
Role:

Schlitz Playhouse (1953)
Episode Title: The Unlighted Road
Role: Jeffrey Latham

Levi's. Un chef d'oeuvre américain.

Levi's

Acknowledgments

Photo & Poster Credits:

David Loehr - The James Dean Gallery - Fairmount, Indiana

Art Harvey, Vintage Posters & Stills - New Jersey

Cinema Collectables - Henderson, Nevada

El Tropico, Movie Star Stills - Isla Verde, P.R.

Cinema Images - Los Angeles, California

Private Designs - New York, New York

Also:

Doug Turiello - He suggested the title of the series The Quest for an Oscar

Martin Grams - Author and host of The Mid-Atlantic Nostalgia
    Convention

James Rosin - Author and actor

Jack Marino - Host of L.A.. Talk Radio, movie producer and director of
    "Forgotten Heroes"

Mike Creager - Host of Amazicon Convention, and dear friend

Koop Kooper - Host of Cocktail Nation Radio Show

Mike Fu - Philosopher and Man of Strength

The entire crew at the Sunset Station Casino, Las Vegas crew: Ron W., Ken,
    Denise, Mike, Arnie, Tommy, Arnold, Bob, Ron the bowler, Paul, Jay,
    Stephen, Brad, Angelo, Hope, Cliff, Whitney and of course Chuck.

Dedicated to Ebie, without her dedication and hard work the book would
have never become reality. Chris Turiello, my son who makes movies!....Doug
Turiello, my son who cooks up a storm and My Dad who would have been
proud!

TEXTURE
sexyhair
stylesexyhair
SLEPT IN
DREAM AS
IF YOU LIVE
FOREVER,
LIVE AS IF
YOU WILL
DIE TODAY.
sexyhair
STYLES CHANGE. SEXY IS FOREVER.
sexyhair.com and professional salons

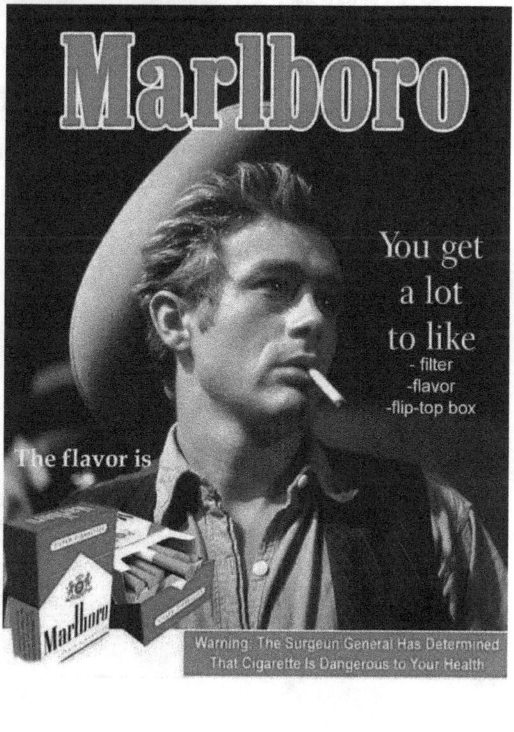
Marlboro
You get
a lot
to like
- filter
-flavor
-flip-top box
The flavor is
Marlboro
Warning: The Surgeun General Has Determined
That Cigarette Is Dangerous to Your Health

James Dean's

first release in over 40 years.
Call for reservations.

He made just three memorable films, so James Dean's flame was brief, but brilliant. And now his legacy is being honored with a special limited-issue commemorative stamp, the second in our Legends of Hollywood series.

The stamp's portrait, created by artist Michael Deas, captures the spirit of James Dean—his defiance, vulnerability, sensitivity and passion. All that made him an actor to watch. And to treasure.

Be first in line for one-of-a-kind James Dean commemoratives —as lasting as the movies he starred in over 40 years ago.

LEGENDS OF HOLLYWOOD

In a brief but brilliant career, the actor, James Dean (1931-1955) spoke for millions of American teenagers as the misunderstood youth in *East of Eden* and *Rebel Without a Cause*. His stature grew mythic after he died in a car crash, shortly before his final film, *Giant*, was completed.

Signed or unsigned Stamp Pane: Cool x 20.

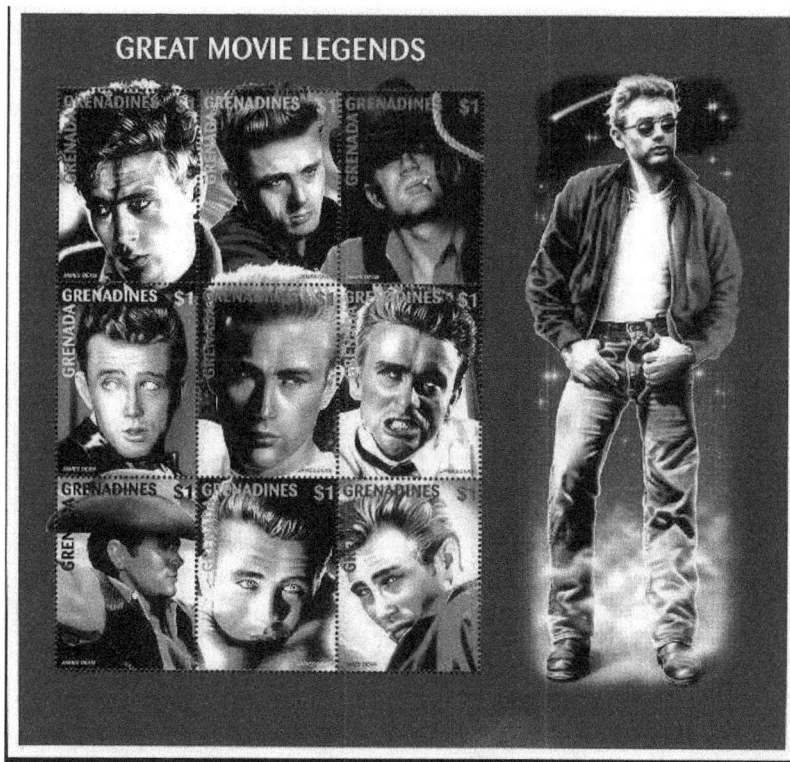

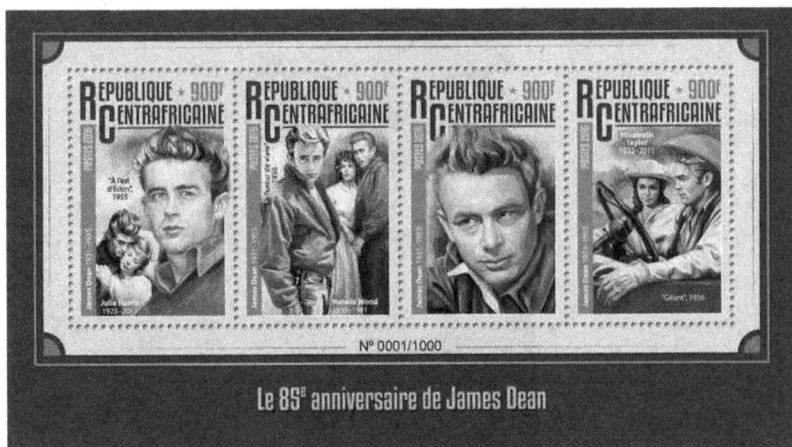

Hollywood Legend

Hollywood Legend

He's back.

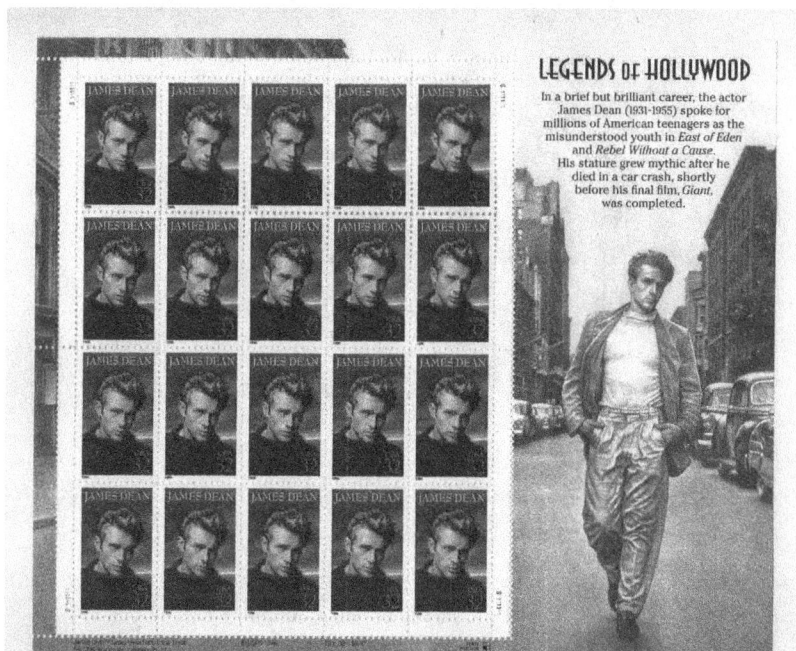

LEGENDS OF HOLLYWOOD

In a brief but brilliant career, the actor James Dean (1931-1955) spoke for millions of American teenagers as the misunderstood youth in *East of Eden* and *Rebel Without a Cause*. His stature grew mythic after he died in a car crash, shortly before his final film, *Giant*, was completed.

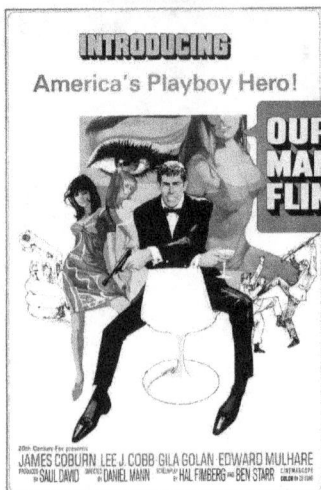

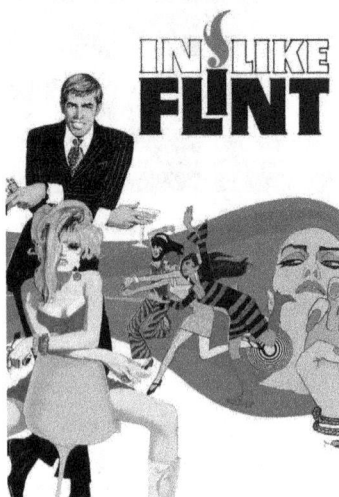

The two greatest spy spoofs ever made, with the only actor who could have played James Bond as good as all the others.

Watch for the next
QUEST FOR AN OSCAR
books coming soon:

Steve McQueen: Quest for an Oscar

Tony Curtis: Quest for an Oscar

Also available from Amazon, Barnes & Noble and everywhere books are sold:

About the Author

Jim Turiello grew up in Washington Heights, New York where his favorite pastimes were playing football, baseball, basketball, and bowling. In his spare time he went to the many movie palaces that were common in upper New York City. He also took the 'A' train to Times Square in the city to catch the latest releases. He claims to have seen all of the following movies over 100 times and these are also his top ten list of great movies. *The Godfather I & II*, *Jaws*, *The Adventures of Robin Hood*, (Errol Flynn version), *King Kong*, (1933), *The Mummy*, (Boris Karloff), *The Creature from the Black Lagoon*, *The Treasure of the Sierra Madre*, *The Thing*, (1951), *Some Like It Hot*, *Rebel Without a Cause*, *Giant*, *Rocky*, *Casino*, *Goodfellas*, *Dirty Harry*...wait a minute that's way more than ten! I guess you are getting the picture, Jim loves movies as well as Flash Gordon and Tim Tyler serials. He had the distinction of being a lead soprano in the world famous St Patrick's Cathedral Choir in New York City.

Jim is an avid football fan of the San Diego Chargers and even writes a weekly sports column for BrianSmithRadio.com. From the 1960's to 2005 he was a regular on numerous sports programs in the tri-state area. As a prolific writer his contributions to music, movie and collectable magazines are too numerous to mention. Jim also produced a unique trading card set, The James Dean Collection, that included 50 photos of James Dean with an original biographical story that ran on the reverse of each card. The card set received rave reviews when it was released and is still available at the James Dean Gallery in Fairmount, Indiana, James Dean's hometown.

Look for the book Jim has been working on for the past twenty years, "The Last Piggyback Ride", a story that will make everyone take notice and will most definitely reach Hollywood as a major motion picture. Jim loves to travel and has been to almost all of the Caribbean Islands but now spends most of his time in Viva Las Vegas. He has two daughters and four sons and lives with his soul mate, Ebie, who coincidentally shares a birthday with Errol Flynn. Marilyn's first dog was named 'Tippy,' the name of her last dog was also named 'Tippy'. When Jim was ten years old his Dad gave him a puppy, Jim decided to call his puppy 'Tippy'. They say you can't make this stuff up.

Errol Flynn: The Quest for an Oscar was Jim's first book in his "Quest for an Oscar" series. It was well received and gave the reader an insight about why Errol deserves to be recognized with an Oscar. Errol's fans were delighted with Jim's approach and were also treated to over 200 photographs. The second "Quest" book about Marilyn Monroe and how she prepared for her roles and was much more serious about perfecting her acting skills will delight her legions of fans. It too has over 200 photographs including artwork and unique programs from around the globe, a big 334 pages. The fourth book in the series The Quest for an Oscar will be about the great actor, Tony

Curtis. In 2018 the author's unpublished novel The Badge in the Tunnel will be released. Jim is hard at work putting together a special Quest for an Oscar book that many readers of the series have suggested. It will be none other than Elvis: The Quest for an Oscar. In the history of motion pictures there has never been a recording icon that was able to make the jump from music to movies so effortlessly.

The author in 1962, really!

The story behind the picture: When Jim was at one of the many conventions, where he was a guest promoting his books, the following incident occurred. Another guest at the convention had a unique photo machine that was able to literally put you in any existing photograph. The gentleman who owned the machine is named, Morton, and when he saw Jim's high school graduation picture, Morton remarked "You look just like Elvis". Jim replied "I know, that was my nickname in high school, college and where-ever I worked". Morton knew Jim was writing a book about Marilyn Monroe and he had a foreign picture of Elvis and Marilyn so he took Jim's graduation picture and substituted Jim in Elvis' place.

There is one more interesting and unbelievable fact regarding the author's Elvis connection. Elvis and Jim both had twin brothers. The twins of Elvis and Jim sadly passed away at birth, a strange but true coincidence.

Jim at a beachfront restaurant that Errol Flynn would have loved to sail to. Turks and Caicos, one of Jim's many ports of call.

Ebie and Jim at the Natural Bridge in Death Valley, 2018.

Eulogy for Hugh Hefner

"I'm very comfortable with the nature of life and death, and that we come to an end. What's most difficult to imagine is that those dreams and early yearnings and desires of childhood and adolescence will also disappear. But who knows? Maybe you become part of the eternal whatever."
- Hugh Hefner

THE WORD LEGEND AND ICONIC are a few of the words that describe Hugh Hefner. The connection he will always have to the author and the author's books is in some ways unique. When the author was a young boy he worked in a candy store In Washington Heights New York. On Saturday nights his job was to put together the Sunday newspapers. Most people think they come complete when they buy them, however each section needs to be added to the front page, the main part. When I was done for the evening each Saturday night the owner of the candy store where I worked allowed me to select any magazine as a bonus. It was an easy choice, Playboy. When the tributes are written about Hef, they may skip over his love for Coke. It was one more thing we had in common. We both only drank Coca-Cola. The famed Playboy mansion had mini refrigerators stocked with Hef's favorite beverage, small green signature Coke bottles. Hef's love of movies was indicative of the weekly movie parties he was so passionate about. Movies gave him joy and inspiration, the author shares that passion. When he gets to his final resting place it will be a special one. Hef will be buried in Westwood Memorial Park in Los Angeles, where he bought the mausoleum drawer next to Marilyn Monroe.

Hugh Hefner, Playboy Magazine and Marilyn Monroe.................

"Never say goodbye because goodbye means going away and going away means forgetting."
........Peter Pan.......

I remember your very first smiles and laughter, the twinkle in your eyes, your tiny hands wrapped around my pinkie....it's your Dad a real life Peter Pan, a tiny little boy that never and will never grow up....for all your dreams..... for you my precious children.....Dawn Marie, James Joseph, Patrick James, Christopher Aaron, Amanda Rose and Douglas Michael....sleep tight......

Final Thoughts

I hope after reading this book you come away with a sense that James Dean was one of the greatest actors of all time. This book focused on his acting and unique persona, only touching on a bibliography of him. There are only three movie performances to evaluate. People who were not around during the time when the three movies were released might have trouble agreeing that he deserved an Oscar. Shakespeare was unique. He got to the heart of the matter, the heart of the story. Shakespeare told about life and death and love and hatred in a way that will last for all time. James Dean captured all those emotions with a style of acting that will never be duplicated. His performances were more than just portrayals of a specific character. He instantly captured your attention by being that character. You wanted to see what he would do next. He was the consummate performer. His early visions were to become a great actor. He succeeded in taking us to places with three special characters. Agatha Christie's most famous novel, *Murder on the Orient Express* has been adapted to the big screen several times. The most recent movie version in 2017 tried to capture the audience once again. This time around the movie was trying too hard. Of course the main attraction was the cast. All of the biggest Hollywood stars of today were assembled to almost guarantee a successful box office hit. Johnny Depp was one of those stars. He might be the closest to James Dean in on screen persona but he might never be able to equal his iconic fame. James Dean would have been exactly the star the lastest adaptation of *Murder on the Orient Express* (2017) needed. The movie is classical much like the three movies James starred in. The truth is we will never know if that observation is correct but it is an interesting challenge.

THE LAST PIGGY BACK RIDE....A STORY ABOUT LOVE......LIFE
AND SORROW......A STORY THAT WILL TOUCH YOUR HEART AND
SOUL......A STORY YOU WILL NEVER FORGET........
..................A TRUE STORY!

The brand new book that will be made into a major motion picture, May
2019 by James Turiello

Index

Bubber Reeves, 257
Buck Rogers, 133
Buckshot, 173
bullfighting, 199
Burr, Raymond, 82, 192
Burton, Richard, 113, 116
Bus Stop, 66
Buzz, 54, 56, 58, 256, 263

C

Caged, 117
Cagney, James, 3, 62, 77, 91, 150
Cagney, Jeanne, 24
Caine Mutiny, The, 37
Cal Trask, 3-4, 115, 187, 201-2, 214, 262
Calabasas California, 56
Cameron, James, 254
Campbell Summer Soundstage, 24, 201, 270
Cape Cod, 254
Captain Blood, 71, 74
Captain Dan Tempest, 161
Captain From Castile, 170

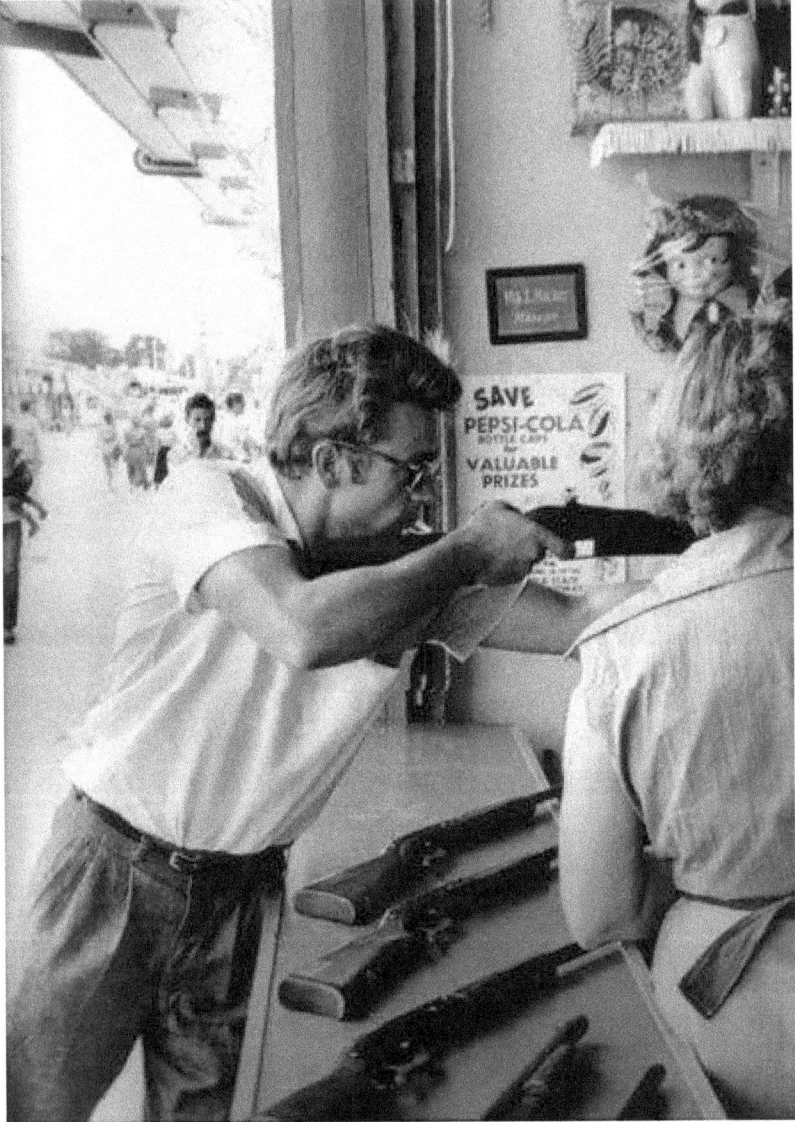

WARNER BROS. STUDIOS
WARDROBE TEST
FOR
#403 GIANT
OF
JAMES DEAN
AS
JETT
(1923)
WARDROBE CHANGE # 3
WORN IN { SET EXT. REATA VERANDA INT. LIBRARY
SCENE 133 - 147
5-21 55

Colorized by TOSHIO.Y

M

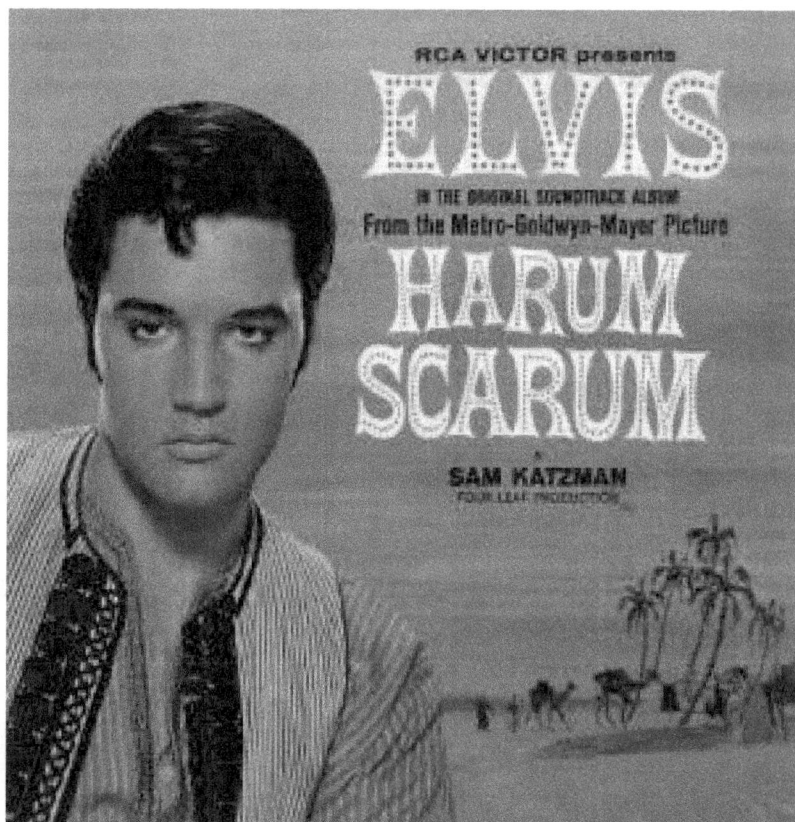

ERROL FLYNN
1909 - 1959

Forgive quickly, kiss
slowly
Love truly, laugh
uncontrollably
And never regret
anything... that makes
you smile.

        - James Dean

www.ingramcontent.com/pod-product-compliance
Lightning Source LLC
Chambersburg PA
CBHW060242100426
42742CB00011B/1615